CATHOLIC PRIMARY RELIGIOUS EDUCATION IN A PLURALIST ENVIRONMENT

Anne Hession is a graduate of Boston College who has lectured in religious education and religious studies at St Patrick's College, Dublin City University, for the past fifteen years. She has recently completed *The Catholic Preschool and Primary School Religious Education Curriculum* (Veritas 2015) for the Irish Episcopal Conference.

Catholic Primary Religious Education in a Pluralist Environment

Anne Hession

VERITAS

Published 2015 by
Veritas Publications
7–8 Lower Abbey Street
Dublin 1, Ireland
publications@veritas.ie
www.veritas.ie

ISBN 978 1 84730 592 3

10 9 8 7 6 5 4 3 2

A catalogue record for this book is available from the British Library.

Designed by Heather Costello, Veritas Publications
Printed by Watermans Printers Ltd, Cork

Veritas books are printed on paper made from the wood pulp of managed forests. For every tree felled, at least one tree is planted, thereby renewing natural resources.

With love to Cathal O'Connell

CONTENTS

SECTION THREE
UNDERSTANDING CATHOLIC PRIMARY RELIGIOUS EDUCATION

Acknowledgements

I would like to acknowledge the support, encouragement and expertise of my colleagues at Saint Patrick's College of Education, Dublin City University, who supported me in this project. I wish to express my gratitude in particular to Cora O' Farrell, Jonathan Kearney, and Andrew O' Shea for sharing their wisdom and expertise with me and for their comments on draft material. I'm also indebted to Caroline Renehan, head of the Department of Religious Studies and Religious Education, who supported me in this venture from the beginning, and who has the rare knack of encouraging the individual strengths of all the people in her team.

I also wish to thank Andrew McGrady, Director Mater Dei Institute of Education, for allowing me to use his work in the glossary. Special thanks to Gráinne Treanor whose proofreading skills greatly enhanced the presentation of the book. Gráinne showed meticulous care and attention to the text, and I very much appreciated her speed, diligence and expertise.

I would like to thank my editor Daragh Reddin and all the staff at Veritas Publications for their comments, suggestions and advice. I would like to acknowledge in particular, Elaine Mahon, Manager of Catechetical Publications, and Maura Hyland, Director of Veritas, for putting their confidence in me and for encouraging me to write this book.

Finally I'd like to thank my fiancé Cathal for believing in me and for encouraging me every step of the way.

INTRODUCTION
CATHOLIC PRIMARY RELIGIOUS EDUCATION IN A PLURALIST ENVIRONMENT

If faithful to its own convictions, Catholic Christianity not only encourages pluralism, it demands it.[1]

MICHAEL HIMES

What is this book about and who is it for?

The book is essentially about religious education in Irish primary schools. It focuses on Catholic religious education and the challenges encountered by Catholic educators. It offers student teachers, diocesan advisors, masters students and teachers in Catholic schools access to a rich tradition of academic thought about religious education, from both outside and inside the Catholic Church community, in a language that is accessible, inviting and relevant. Catholic religious education is presented as one important approach to primary religious education in a society that welcomes differing types of religious education. The author believes in the possibility of harmonious co-existence between adherents of different approaches to religious education and welcomes the creation through dialogue of an educational environment in which differing approaches to religious education can flourish.

In the past few years, we have witnessed the development of increasing recognition, in Irish society and at European level, of the importance of the moral, spiritual and religious dimensions of education. This growing awareness serves as an important counterpoint to the emphasis on a concept of education that meets economic needs and values human persons solely on the basis of their potential contribution to 'the knowledge economy' and to economic and social development in general. For the student teacher and, indeed, practising teachers in Irish primary schools, the questions might arise: what distinguishes the academic discipline of religious education from subjects such as ethical education, intercultural education, human rights education, citizenship education and social personal and health education (SPHE)? What do the differing forms of religious education contribute to the overall education and personal development of the child and what do they contribute to society as a whole?

This book distinguishes the Catholic approach to religious education from alternative approaches, for students who are being introduced to different approaches concurrently during the course of initial teacher education programmes. What are the underpinning theological principles and educational perspectives that inform Catholic approaches to primary religious education? Is it possible to sustain a commitment to Catholic education while supporting and upholding the values of the liberal democratic society in which we live? Does a Catholic perspective have anything to contribute to the search for a healthy pluralism in society? How does education in the Catholic faith relate to and differ from other forms of religious education that might be offered in schools? What is the current curriculum of religious education for Irish Catholic primary schools? This primer in Catholic education seeks to empower students and practising teachers to pose and explore those questions.

What is the aim of the book?

The book aims to present the vision of the person and the way of life which Catholic primary education seeks to promote, with particular attention to the type of school-based religious education which contributes to this vision, in a respectful and constructive dialogue with other visions of education and, in particular, with other approaches to religious education currently offered in liberal western democracies.

The Bengali poet and Hindu, Rabindranath Tagore, held that proper teaching does not explain things; proper teaching stokes curiosity.[2] Thus, while the author cannot hope to avoid the temptation to explain, this book is first and foremost an attempt to stoke the curiosity of student teachers of Catholic education. Its first concern is to whet the appetite of these students as they delve (many of them for the first time) into the academic discipline of religious education and the rich philosophical and theological tradition of Catholic education. The book recognises the very real tensions experienced by young student-teachers immersed in the values of Irish society who are invited to teach in schools whose values do not completely align with societal practices and perspectives. Those academics responsible for introducing these students to the discipline of Catholic religious education are challenged to make real connections between the assumptions of the differing worldviews of most of their students and the unique perspective that Catholic education offers.

The book does not pretend to explore or present all the rich theological and philosophical insights and perspectives on Catholic education found in the Catholic Church's teaching. Nor will it explore the whole issue of ethos and the 'Catholic' ethos of schools, or the growing academic debate on the justification for faith-based schools. There are other books and documents which do that. (See suggested supplementary reading at the end of Chapters One and Two.) Instead, this book aims to help student teachers to begin to understand the Catholic vision of education and of religious education within the context of some alternative models of education and of religious and ethical education offered in the Irish and British contexts. To this end, the book aims to offer students some basic signposts to the literature, helping them to understand the political, theological, philosophical and educational perspectives that inform public discourse on primary religious education in Ireland at this time.

What is the language of this book?

This book draws on the Catholic tradition of religious education and on the civic educational discourse in the domain of primary religious education that is now emerging in the Irish context. In other words, the book is written on the premise that there is a difference between the 'in-house' Catholic Church language of religious education and the language of religious education used in the public square. This book uses both languages, because teachers in Catholic schools need to be conversant in both. As the education philosophers, Terence McLaughlin and Hanan Alexander, have explained, 'Liberal democratic societies require their citizens to engage in public or civic forms of reasoning as well as those that are internal to their own substantial vision of the good'.[3]

Catholic educators need to be rooted in the wisdom of their own religious tradition in such a way that hope in and commitment to the educational vision of the Christian community is continually renewed. When the Catholic educational community develops strong conversations about its own values, commitments and traditions, Catholic teachers can come to the public square as full conversational partners. But Catholic teachers also need to be able to engage in dialogue with people in the public arena who espouse differing philosophies of education and, in particular, with those who advocate differing approaches to religious and/or ethical education. Any adequate discourse on religious education in Ireland today must empower Catholic teachers to participate in both conversations at once and give them the tools to move between the conversations.

A new discourse for primary religious education

In Ireland, we are witnessing the development of a new discourse on primary religious education in a public as opposed to an ecclesial space.[4] One impetus for this development is the growing recognition that the rights of *all* children to a spiritual, moral and religious education have not been adequately honoured in Irish primary education thus far.[5] Irish academics qualified in religious education are now beginning to articulate the educational foundations of the public discipline of religious education, which includes, but need not be limited to, theological contributions to the understanding of the discipline. The first step in developing a common language for primary religious education is to explore the question of what children can *learn from* religion, in which the principal objective becomes the question of what religious education contributes to young children's spiritual, moral and religious development.[6] A second step in developing this common language is to discern which types of religious education will best contribute to children's healthy engagement with pluralism and diversity in Irish society.

Responding to plurality

There seems to be a developing consensus, both in Ireland and at European level, that one of the goals of religious education, wherever it is carried out, is to promote a healthy religious, spiritual and ethical pluralism in society.[7] Here *plurality* is used as a descriptive term that refers to the actual cultural and religious diversity present in Irish society. While Ireland has always been diverse, increasing immigration into Ireland from the 1990s onwards has led to an increase in the number of people espousing differing religious and ethical worldviews. Coupled with this, in the context of a globalised world, children are more than ever before exposed to a plurality of ideas, values, models and alternative stances for living. As L. Philip Barnes reminds us, the term religious diversity need not apply only to diversity between religions; diversity is also a feature within religions.

> Ironically, new forms of diversity have resulted not just from the process of (what sociologists call) individualisation, whereby meaning and identity in a culture shift from institutions and structures to the self who chooses from a range of identities, but also as a consequence of globalisation, either as a critical

reaction to it or as the cultivation of minority identities that are facilitated by digital forms of communication. The challenge for education and schools in this context is to provide pupils with the knowledge and skills to construct their own identities from the diverse and often contradictory materials of culture.[8]

In other words, because of an increasing pluralism of worldviews or religions, together with the forces of modernisation and globalisation, the process of identity formation in contemporary Irish society has become a lot more complex than for earlier generations, with people integrating multiple perspectives and contradictory rationalities into a more reflexive, contextual and plural identity. This process of pluralisation implies, as Lieven Boeve, explains:

that each identity is structurally challenged to conceive of itself in relation to difference and otherness – especially to the effect of other truth claims to its own claim. This is a necessary step to be taken by all religious positions, and has also implications for the organisation of the public realm in a multicultural society. It is precisely here that the question of equal and mutual recognition of religious positions poses itself, and where the different reactions of intolerance, passive and active tolerance manifest themselves.[9]

The question arises, in such a context, as to whether it is possible or even desirable to educate for a particular religious identity any more. Is it possible for a child to grow up with a strong Christian or other religious worldview in such a way that this identity proves capable of sustaining a healthy spirituality throughout his/her life in multi-cultural societies? Is education in a strongly rooted religious or other cultural identity even something to be desired in a world of diversity and rapid change? Is there a place within the European context for forms of religious education which take religion seriously as the source of 'ultimate concern' and of comprehensive meaning in people's lives?[10]

The author believes that it is possible to educate for a positive concept of Catholic identity and indeed that healthy rootedness in particular spiritual traditions is necessary if children are to negotiate the complexity of the world they now inhabit. However, the context in which such education is carried out has changed forever. Today, educating for Catholic religious identity and educating for responsible pluralism must be understood as intrinsically related concerns.[11] In other words, given the complexity of the process of identity formation in contemporary society, Catholics will not only be concerned with the credibility of their worldview in the midst of competing worldviews; they will also be concerned with how children will live out their particular religious identity in a diverse society. It may be that they will have to teach their children two languages – the 'in-house' language of their own tradition and the public language of religion – and the next generation will have to be conversant in both if Christian identity is to be a viable option for future generations. In any case, a huge shift of consciousness is now required of Catholic educators: 'to set the Church and its educational work in the context of encounter with diverse religious and non-religious worlds'.[12]

Educating for tolerance, respect and social cohesion

There seems to be a general consensus among Irish educators that religious and ethical difference should not only be allowed or tolerated in schools, but that children should be taught to value difference and to learn from it. However, an important question now facing Irish primary education is what kind of religious and/or ethical education will actually bring about mutual respect, tolerance and appreciation of religions and beliefs? In this regard, it is very important to distinguish descriptions of plurality and a pluralist society from normative statements about how one should respond to the fact of diversity and the complexity of identity formation in a postmodern world. Lieven Boeve makes this important point when he writes that '... in the discussion unnoticed shifts often occur between analysis and evaluation, between "description" of the current context and a "programme" to deal with it'.[13]

An unexamined shift from description to programme has suggested to some that active-pluralist non-confessional religious education is the best alternative for all Irish primary schools. As Terrence Merrigan observes, 'the more or less self-evident character of the transition from the recognition that the contemporary culture is pluralistic to the option for an educational model based on pluralist theology is remarkable'.[14] The danger inherent in such a move, argues Merrigan, is that a subtle shift occurs from (epistemological) pluralism as an acceptance of the right of religions and beliefs to exist, to an ideological pluralism that has, as its ultimate goal, 'the neutralisation of all heterogeneity by the imposition of a totalitarian understanding of truth. In this scenario, there is only one truth, namely, the truth of pluralism'.[15]

Any worthy affirmation of pluralism, Merrigan argues, must take plurality seriously, acknowledging real and even insurmountable differences between religions and worldviews, recognising that respect for pluralism is 'not incompatible with commitment to the irreducible particularity' of a religious tradition and that 'such commitment does not vitiate the possibility of authentic interreligious encounter (or dialogue)'.[16] Peta Goldburg has argued in a similar vein, saying that genuine pluralism should not require of children that they relinquish their particular religious, spiritual or ethical commitments. It should allow them to be distinctly themselves in relationship to others and be clear about their differences from others while affirming their similarities.[17]

An opportunity to put children first

As a new public language of religious education is developed for primary level, it will be important to remember that, logically and psychologically, there is a difference between primary and secondary education and that the spiritual, ethical and religious needs of young children differ in some important ways to that of adolescents and adults. Religious education responds to a natural questioning about reality and is unavoidably set within a developmental context. Some models of religious education assume a capacity for critical rational thought that many young children simply have not developed yet. They depend, in other words, on children having reached 'formal operational thinking', the capacity to think abstractly, and articulate an understanding of complex beliefs and compare worldviews and religions.[18] This emphasis on critical reason and rational autonomy is questionable. Critical reason is not the most important principle in the religious education of young children. Discovering and understanding the language and content of religious traditions, exploring the narrative and experiential dimensions of religions, communicating basic religious beliefs, opening to wonder, and use of the imagination are more important than critical reason and the growing emphasis on rational autonomy in the early years.

Another danger is the temptation to reduce the role of religious education in the curriculum to the social, political and moral goals of education. To do so runs the risk of excluding the transcendent, the role of ritual, texts and narratives, and the production of meaning arising from these in religions. Furthermore, there is a danger in religious communities being required to conform their religious education curricula to the requirements of public ethics, thus pushing all other dimensions of their religious traditions into the private sphere.[19] Religion and the religious should not be reduced to the political goals of social cohesion, diversity and plurality, so that the link between religious education and the religious life is lost.[20]

Religious education justifies its place on the primary school curriculum by the contribution it makes to children's personal development. This requires a profound engagement with actual children's lives. This does not mean that religious learning should be reduced to the experience and psychological needs of the learner or that the language of religious education should be reduced to the language of social science (though that is important too!)[21] Nor does it deny the nature of religion as something that addresses the child with a call, a gift and a challenge. It does mean, however, that educators pay attention to young children's actual capacities for religious knowledge and the kinds of knowing or skills of religious literacy that will genuinely enhance their spiritual, moral and religious lives as children. In sum, religious education for young children must be age-sensitive. It must take the actual cognitive capacities, and the social, emotional and spiritual maturity of children seriously, while working with their own natural ability to learn and grow, to question reality and to remain open to ultimate meaning.

Finally, the religious education of young children will take their communities of belief and their lived experience of community seriously. One of the primary needs of the small child is for a sense of belonging and all those charged with their education will seek to create a harmonious synergy between the culture of the home and the school-based educational experience of the child. There seems to be broad agreement that this is the case. However, there is a significant dearth of sociological and cultural research on children's lived experiences of religious and other stances for living in Ireland.

Catholic religious education: what has changed?

The recent focus on primary religious education with the publication of *The Forum on Patronage and Pluralism in the Primary Sector: Report of the Forum's Advisory Group* (April 2012) has stimulated fresh dialogue and debate within the Catholic educational community about the distinctive nature of Catholic schools and of the particular values and commitments that they bring to primary education in Ireland. Many Catholic schools are currently engaging in a process of reflection and evaluation with a view to clarifying their vision and goals.[22] One important positive outcome of this process has been an attempt to discern how Catholic schools' stated commitment to the inclusion of non-Catholic students can be improved in terms of concrete practices and policies.[23]

The socio-cultural context within which Catholic schools operate has changed radically in the past ten to twenty years. Many Catholic educators are now working in a secular environment in which the Christian worldview is alternatively affirmed and challenged. For some children in schools and for some teachers as well, Christian faith is no longer the only perspective from which they understand the world and their role in it. Concern about challenges to the Christian worldview is a key element of the 1998 statement by the Catholic Congregation for Education, *The Catholic School on the Threshold of the Third Millennium*. The document states that among the many problems facing Catholic schools is that, in countries of long-standing Christianity, there is 'a growing marginalisation of the Christian faith as a reference point and a source of light for an effective and convincing interpretation of existence'.[24] In its discussion notes, a recent synod of bishops explained that, '[i]n our times, we find ourselves in an era of a profound secularism which has led to a loss in the capacity to listen and understand the words of the Gospel as a living and life-giving message. ... Temptations to superficiality and self-centredness, arising from a predominating hedonistic and consumer-oriented mentality, are not easily overcome'.[25]

The inclusive enrolment policies of Catholic schools in the Republic of Ireland has led to another important change. As Siebrem Miedema and Gert Biesta note:

> The situation in denominational schools has changed as a result of the fact that most of these schools have become more open with respect to their admittance policy. This means that they can no longer assume that the school is simply an extension of the normative and religious or (broader speaking) worldview orientation of the families where their students come from. A more plural society has led to a much more plural school population in both denominational and non-denominational schools. ... Schools can neither maintain that they are value-free zones of instruction, nor can they claim that their normative 'message' is simply an extension of what happens in the sphere of the family. [26]

To summarise, Catholic school managers can no longer make assumptions about the beliefs and values of students or of teachers in Catholic schools. Nor can they assume that educational solutions devised in a time when Catholic primary religious education and catechesis were indistinguishable will be appropriate for the current Irish context.[27] There is an urgent need for theories of religious education that meet the needs of teachers and students within the cultural reality of Irish Catholic primary schools. As Sandra Cullen rightly points out, 'an explicit educational theory of the relationship between religious education as a faith activity and religious education that is adequate or appropriate for the classroom on educational grounds, or on the grounds of public interest, has not yet evolved'.[28]

Content of the book
This book is divided into three sections. The first section, entitled 'Understanding Catholic Education', introduces readers to two of the discourses engaged in by professionals

when discussing Catholic education. Chapter One introduces the language of *philosophy* and invites readers to look at schooling types from a philosophical perspective. The chapter draws the reader's attention to the fact that all schools (implicitly or explicitly) offer students differing philosophical modes of life and spiritualities. The argument is made that, while both Educate Together and Catholic schools share a common framework of values consistent with a concern for intellectual, moral and spiritual liberty, democracy, social justice and human rights, these schools differ significantly on what is considered 'full personal development' or 'wholeness' or on what kind of transformation is considered permissible or possible in education. Catholic and Educate Together philosophies of education are compared in terms of the priority given to certain virtues and values, the understanding of the person and worldview proposed by the schools, and the different ways the purpose or goal of schooling is understood. This chapter introduces readers to the distinctiveness of a Catholic philosophy of education as the context within which Catholic religious education is carried out.

Chapter Two introduces students to the language of *theology* as another academic discourse which informs Catholic education. Faith in God is the ultimate educational foundation for Catholic schools. By focusing on the central themes of God, Jesus and Church, readers are offered a springboard for their own reading of the Catholic documents on education and the academic literature on faith-based education in general. A Catholic school is described as a school which offers a holistic view of education, which celebrates God's reign, places relationship with Jesus Christ at the centre, and builds a community serving the mission of the Church in the world. Some educational implications of this understanding are then explored and readers are invited to reflect on the ways teachers' Christian theological commitments might impact on their educational praxis in schools.

The second section is entitled 'Towards a Public Language of Religious Education for Primary Level'. The intention in this section is to contribute to the development of a civic language of religious education for the primary sector in Ireland – one which will allow for the respectful accommodation of differing approaches to the discipline in denominational, multi-denominational and non-denominational school environments. Chapter Three aims to describe the discipline of religious education, drawing on the academic language of religious education used by those engaged in the discipline at European and international levels. The argument is made that the way religious education is carried out in any school reflects particular understandings of *religion* and of *education*. One understanding of religion is proposed as the basis for developing a common language for the academic discipline of religious education in the Irish context, wherever it is practised. This understanding of religious education aims to respect the distinctive contribution of *religion* to education. Finally, the issue of indoctrination is examined and the international perspective within which all religious education in Irish primary schools should be carried out is introduced.

Following the work of Hanan Alexander and Terence H. McLaughlin, Chapter Four distinguishes between two main approaches to religious education found in pluralist liberal democracies: 'education in religion and spirituality from the inside' and 'education in religion and spirituality from the outside'. These two approaches are described and some of the possible strengths and weaknesses of both approaches are outlined. The argument is made that all forms of religious and spiritual education should allow young children to begin to develop a deep appreciation and understanding of their own religion or life stance, but which also encourage genuine engagement and dialogue with people of differing religious faiths and other stances for living.[29] Ideally, all children should be educated in ways conducive to the development of healthy spiritual and/or religious identities *and* to a positive approach to religious and spiritual pluralism, regardless of the schooling type they attend.

The third section of the book is entitled 'Understanding Catholic Primary Religious Education'. Chapter Five offers an introduction to religious education in Irish Catholic Primary Schools. Catholic religious education is presented as a form of religious education that supports the development of a distinctive religious identity in the context of diversity – one that is simultaneously distinctive and inclusive, rooted and open, committed and tolerant, receptive and enquiring. As such it is argued that Catholic primary religious education should pursue the tasks of formation and critical education as complementary tasks at every level of the curriculum. Further, the chapter demonstrates that, when religion is approached as a lived response to God's loving presence and action in people's lives, it impacts upon the kinds of curricular activities that are valued. The nature of Christian faith, in its cognitive, affective and behavioural dimensions, shapes the skills and 'ways of knowing' we utilise in our attempt to teach and understand it.

Chapter Six provides an introduction to the Catholic Pre-school and Primary School Religious Education Curriculum. The theological rationale underpinning Catholic religious education is distinguished from the educational language of the curriculum which describes educational aims, outcomes, skills of religious literacy, knowledge and concepts, assessment strategies and pedagogical approaches. The chapter raises the question of what it means for a child to be religiously literate in the Catholic faith, and five different dimensions of religious literacy which are emphasised in the Catholic tradition are outlined. The four interrelated strands – Christian Faith, The Word of God, Liturgy/Prayer and Christian Morality – are then described. Together, these four strands outline the knowledge and understanding, skills and processes that make up the learning to be achieved at each level of the curriculum. Finally, the reason religious education outcomes are distinguished from faith formation goals in the curriculum is discussed.

The final chapter offers some introductory reflections on Catholic moral education. This chapter introduces some distinctive features of a Catholic approach to moral education at primary level, in the context of alternative ethical approaches. Some common misunderstandings about the Catholic moral education of young children are examined and some distinctive features of the 'Christian Morality' strand of the Catholic Primary Religious Education Curriculum are outlined. A set of questions for reflection and some suggestions for supplementary reading are offered at the end of each chapter.

Introduction

Endnotes

1. Michael J. Himes, 'Catholicism as Integral Humanism: Christian Participation in Pluralistic Moral Education' in F. Clark Power and Daniel K. Lapsley (eds), *The Challenge of Pluralism: Education, Politics and Values* (Notre Dame: University of Notre Dame Press, 1992), 117–39.

2. K. Dutta and A. Robinson, *Rabindranath Tagore: The Myriad-Minded Man* (New York: Saint Martin's Press, 1995), 50.

3. Hanan Alexander and Terence H. McLaughlin, 'Education in Religion and Spirituality' in N. Blake, P. Smeyers, R. Smith and P. Standish (eds),*The Blackwell Guide to the Philosophy of Education* (Oxford: Blackwell, 2003), 371.

4. Anne Looney maps the progress of Irish secondary level religious education from the ecclesial to the public space in 'Religious Education in the Public Space: Challenges and contestations' in M. de Souza et al. (eds), *International Handbook of the Religious, Moral and Spiritual Dimensions in Education* (Dordrecht: Springer, 2006), 949–66. Sandra Cullen provides an interesting introduction to the four publics to which religious education has to be accountable: the State, the Church, the academy and the person. Sandra Cullen, 'Toward an Appropriate Religious Education for Future Teachers of Religious Education: Principles for a Theological Education Approach', Doctoral Thesis, Dublin City University, July 2013, unpublished.

5. For a reflection on an experience of exclusion from the perspective of Atheist Ireland, see Michael Nugent and Jane Donnelly, 'Only Secular Schools Respect Every Person's Human Rights Equally' in Gareth Byrne and Patricia Kieran (eds), *Toward Mutual Ground: Pluralism, Religious Education and Diversity in Irish Schools* (Dublin: The Columba Press, 2013), 187–95.

6. The terms 'learning religion', 'learning about religion' and 'learning from religion' were first used by Michael Grimmitt. See Michael Grimmitt, *Religious Education and Human Development* (Great Wakering, Essex, England: McCrimmon Publishing Co. LTD, 1987), 225.

7. The development of concepts of European identity and active citizenship has introduced another layer to the model of relationships with which the school is now engaged. See the Inter-European Commission on Church and School (ICCS) Working Group, 'Giving Europe a Heart and Soul – A Christian Vision for Education in Europe's Schools', in Peter Schreiner, Hans Spinder, Jeremy Taylor and Wim Westerman (eds), *Committed to Europe's Future: contributions from Education and Religious Education: a Reader* (Münster: Comenius Institute, 2002), 79–84.

8. L. Philip Barnes, 'Diversity' in L. Philip Barnes (ed.), *Debates in Religious Education* (London: Routledge, 2012), 68–9.

9. Lieven Boeve, 'Religious Education in a post-secular and post-Christian context', *Journal of Beliefs & Values* (2012), 33(2): 146.

10. For a reflection on this question, see Terrence Merrigan, 'Religion, Education and the Appeal to Plurality: Theological Considerations on the Contemporary European Context' in Byrne and Kieran (eds), ibid., 57–70.

11. Fayette Breaux Veverka, 'Practicing Faith: Negotiating identity and Difference in a religiously pluralistic world', *Religious Education* (2004), 99(1): 38–55.

12. Kieran Scott, 'Three Traditions of Religious Education' in Jeff Astley and Leslie J. Francis (eds), *Critical Perspectives on Christian Education: A reader on*

the aims, principles and philosophy of Christian education (Gracewing Publishing, 1994), 287.

13. Lieven Boeve, 'Religious Education in a post-secular and post-Christian context', *Journal of Beliefs & Values* (2012) 33(2):145.

14. Merrigan, ibid., 67.

15. Merrigan, ibid., 66.

16. Merrigan, ibid., 68. For the argument that an attitude of intolerance does not logically follow from belief in the uniqueness and superiority of one's own religion, see L. Philip Barnes, *Education, Religion and Diversity* (London: Routledge, 2014), 146–52.

17. Peta Goldburg, 'Developing Pedagogies for Inter-religious Teaching and Learning' in K. Engebretson et al. (eds), *International Handbook of Inter-Religious Education* (Dordrecht: Springer, 2010), 356.

18. Jean Piaget, *The Psychology of Intelligence* (Totowa, NJ: Littlefield, 1972).

19. On the emergence of new forms of civic religious discourse in European and American funded projects on religious education, see Liam Gearon, *Masterclass in Religious Education: transforming teaching and learning* (London: Bloomsbury, 2013) 29–45. For reservations about use of the discourse of citizenship and rights in religious education see Barnes, *Education Religion and Diversity*, Chapter 14.

20. On the ways in which the political interest manifest in religion has impacted on understandings of religious education and on the dangers of the over-politicisation of religion and the reduction of religion to utilitarian principles, see Gearon, ibid., 132 and passim.

21. I am opposed to the idea that education should be completely reduced to what is psychologically, physically or socially *needed* by the person. An ontological assessment of the person is also necessary for a sound philosophy of education.

22. In March 2015, the Catholic Schools Partnership published a booklet resource for Catholic Schools in developing policies that will foster best practice with regard to the inclusion of all pupils. *Catholic Schools Partnership, Catholic Primary Schools in a Changing Ireland: Sharing good practice on inclusion of all pupils,* (Maynooth; Catholic Schools Partnership, 2015).

23. There are some Catholic schools which have been exemplary in this regard, but a wider sharing of ideas and practices among Catholic schools is needed. See Maurice Ryan's discussion of the implications of inclusive, exclusive and pluralist approaches to Catholic education in his 'Including students who are not Catholics in Catholic schools' in Stephen McKinney (ed.), *Faith Schools in the Twenty-first Century* (Edinburgh: Dunedin Academic Press, 2008), 30–40. In July 2014, Minister for Education Ruairi Quinn, T.D. published a paper (*Forum on Patronage and Pluralism in the Primary Sector: Progress to Date and Future Directions*) which outlines examples of how schools are working to respect the rights of pupils of all faiths and none, while still remaining true to the ethos of the school. Available on www.education.ie.

24. Congregation for Catholic Education, *The Catholic school on the threshold of the third millennium,* 1998, no.1.

25. Synod of Bishops, XIII Ordinary General Assembly, 'The New Evangelization for the Transmission of the Christian Faith', 2011. Available on the Vatican website, http://www.vatican.va.

26. Siebren Miedema and Gert J. J. Biesta, 'Instruction or Educating for Life? On the aims of religiously-affiliated schools and others' in *International Journal of Education and Religion* (2003), 4(1): 89

27. The terms 'catechesis', 'Christian religious education', 'religious education', and 'religious instruction' continue to be used interchangeably by many writing about Catholic religious education. To do so ignores the significant conceptual gap between differing types of religious education, and important differences in the contexts in which this religious education is carried out. As G. P. Fleming points out, there is no single meaning for the terms 'catechesis' and 'religious education' even in Church documents and an uncritical transference of terms from one context to another is to be avoided. G. P. Fleming, 'Catholic Church Documents on Religious Education' in M. de Souza et al. (eds), ibid., 608ff. For a helpful proposal on usage of terms in the Irish context, see Andrew McGrady, 'Teaching Religion' in Gareth Byrne and Patricia Kieran (eds), ibid., 79–94.

28. Many Church catechetical documents generally provide principles of pastoral theology rather than educational theory as such. Sandra Cullen, *Toward an Appropriate Religious Education for Future Teachers of Religious Education: Principles for a Theological Education Approach,* Doctoral thesis 2013, Mater Dei Institute of Education, A College of Dublin City University, Unpublished, 105.

29. See Mary C. Boys and Sara S. Lee, *Christians and Jews in dialogue: learning in the presence of the other* (Woodstock, ON: Skylight Paths, 2006).

SECTION ONE
UNDERSTANDING CATHOLIC EDUCATION

CHAPTER ONE
PARTICULARITY AND PLURALISM: EDUCATIONAL PHILOSOPHIES IN IRISH PRIMARY SCHOOLS

Children grow into responsible adults through their engagement with communities of meaning. Communities of meaning successfully reproduce themselves by preserving and passing on to their children a cultural memory – their story, their identity, their cultural anchor points – and a cultural vision – their imagined future and their worldview and life view, which help them explain the arc of their lives and the arc of history. Such memory and vision can provide motivation and meaning for a lifetime. The full expression of those cultural dimensions, memory and vision, shapes people into a community. The full expression of those dimensions in an individual shapes his or her identity. If a community is to survive, if individuals are to survive, both memory and vision must be preserved and passed on.[1]

STEVEN C. VRYHOF

Every education teaches a philosophy; if not by dogma then by suggestion, by implication, by atmosphere. Every part of that education has a connection with every other part. If it does not all combine to convey some general view of life, it is not education at all.[2]

G. K. CHESTERTON

One evening as I was helping my five-year-old daughter brush her teeth, she suddenly pushed the toothbrush out of her mouth and asked: 'Why am I, I am?' Then, with a broad sweep of her two arms she asked, 'And why is this all here?' That these were serious questions for her could be in no doubt. They are spiritual questions, questions that go to the heart of her developing sense of self as a unique person as well as her sense of the purpose of her life in the world. When my daughter asked these questions, I could have given her a purely scientific explanation about the evolution of the world and the place of human beings within it. Alternatively, I could have explained to her that she was made by God and that she had a unique purpose in the world that God created. Whatever answer I gave I was implicitly conveying and teaching her a distinct perspective on what is true – a particular way of understanding the world and her role in it. I was communicating my understanding of the nature and purpose of human life to her. What's more, this communication was inevitable. I could not teach her to stand upon some 'neutral ground' from which she could assess all the possible answers to her questions. She needed me to tell her what I thought to be true.

As small children we all learn to interpret our experience through one particular lens or paradigm and we all must begin with some worldview or other. This worldview is usually that of our parents. They teach us a certain way of understanding ourselves, others and the world around us. They model a certain way of being in the world that we absorb such that it becomes normal and common sense. Our worldview will say something about reality (the way things are), about whether reality is basically good or trustworthy, about the purpose of human life, about what

36

we can know, about what it means to live a good life, and about the ultimate destiny of human beings.[3]

Education and the meaning of life

In a similar fashion, all school-based education forms children in certain clearly identifiable values, virtues and beliefs, and all teachers work with some understanding (often implicit, sometimes explicit) of reality, of the person and of the purpose of human life.[4] Another way of understanding this is to say that every school ultimately teaches children something relatively consistent about the important questions that all people must face in their lives: Is it good to be alive? Does life have a purpose or meaning? Do I give my own life a meaning or is my life's meaning given to me? Is the human being matter or spirit or both? Is the human person essentially an individual or is relationship with others and with God an intrinsic part of personhood? Do I have a soul and what difference does that make to how I live my life? Is living a happy human life the whole story or is there something which matters beyond life, on which life itself is dependent? Does it really matter what I commit myself to? Is my life to be lived purely for myself or for others and why? Who or what guides my moral decisions, the kind of person I think I should be and the kind of society I want to help create? What if I fail in life? What about evil, suffering, tragedy and death? The answers given to these questions reveal the vision of human life or the philosophy of education proposed by any particular school.

Education as a way of life

John L. Elias proposes that the ultimate purpose of education is 'the adoption of a particular way of life in company with others'.[5] Good education teaches students the art of living or 'how life is to be lived'.[6] Unfortunately, in our time, many commentators in government, business, the media and even the educational establishment seem to understand education as a commodity that delivers the goals of social and economic policy laid down by government. This is manifest, for example, in the relentless emphasis on market-driven success, on predetermined, measurable outcomes, skills and competencies, on technical expertise and accountability criteria. This 'marketisation' of education has become so ubiquitous that Pádraig Hogan laments that 'the question of the relationship between learning and how one ought to live is already answered in much of the new official discourse on the learning society'.[7] The capacity of creative human beings to act in ways that are fundamentally new or different seems to be missing here.

Education as transformation

What seems to be getting lost in much of the current discourse on education is that good education is not merely about the acquisition of skills and information (though these are important in themselves), but aims for the personal development and transformation of the *whole* person.[8] Good education is essentially about the development of good characters: people who know how to discern what is true and good, people who are developing a consistency between what they know and believe, their feelings, their attitudes, their values and their actions in the world. Such a person is not only skilled; they are *wise*. They are persons who are attuned to the connections between their minds, their bodies and their spirits. As Anne Hunt explains, the educated person is not only able to understand the world and qualified to play her part in the society in which she lives; 'she is also attuned to the deepest desires of the human heart and their ultimate quest and fulfilment'.[9] These desires are for happiness, for truth, for justice, for beauty, and for a sense of meaning and purpose in life.

Well-educated persons tend to be grounded in a strong sense of self or identity which enables them to respond freely and responsibly to all they meet. They are persons who value the development of their intellectual life *in itself* and not merely as a means to economic or even social ends. Further, they value ways of knowing such as the aesthetic and the spiritual that do not have any obvious monetary and productive values, but which are nevertheless crucial for living life well. Such persons have developed the wisdom to know how to use their knowledge and skills in ways which benefit every person in the world and the created environment.

Each school type differs on what is considered 'holistic' personal development or on what kind of transformation is considered permissible or possible in education. A secular school, for example, may take its vision/image of the human person from a more rational social science and from liberal philosophy. A faith-based school might integrate the insights of the social sciences and philosophy with the understanding of the person offered by the humanities, and particularly theology, which attempts to bring a more creative relational approach to the whole person. Thus, the essential difference between a Catholic school and a secular school goes far beyond the presence or absence of religious education or even the type of religious or ethical education on offer. The entire educational philosophy of each school is based on a radically different understanding of reality, of the person and of the purpose of human life.

Educational narratives and culture

All educational philosophies are situated in particular cultures. However strong a school's philosophy is, the cultures children are immersed in offer compatible or rival understandings of the nature of human life. The culture we live in forms our perceptive system, its languages and symbols mould our thought, and a certain way of looking at reality can dominate a society to such an extent that it becomes unquestioned and seems like common sense.[10] For example, those of us who live in liberal Western democracies will place a high value on tolerance of individual difference and so a culture that enshrines the values of liberty and equality, and an ethical environment which stresses the importance of self-esteem and personal responsibility, will hardly need justification in our eyes. In a similar fashion, the concept of authority and particularly of religious authority is becoming less acceptable to contemporary Western consciousness, with its emphasis on the autonomy of the individual over and against all institutions and authorities. Thus many people today tend to be sceptical when faced with what are perceived as hegemonic claims to truth or to moral superiority or authority.

In any case, the fact is that children do not just encounter *spiritualities*, differing ethical frameworks or philosophies of life at school. Such encounters permeate the very cultural air that children breathe and it acts on the young child's imagination as powerfully as any explicit religious or secular framework, perhaps even more powerfully for being implicit. As Michael Warren explains:

> Both religion and the wider culture claim the meanings they propose are the ultimate ones. The wider culture ...

makes its claims to ultimacy *covertly*; a religious system makes its claims overtly. The problem is that the covert claims can be more powerful because, never explicitly made, they are harder to identify and resist. ... [T]he wider culture forms us, creates in us habits of the heart and dispositions needed by the economic system, and we tend, not just to overlook what is happening, but to be unable to notice.[11]

The values of unfettered capitalism, materialism and consumerism run contrary to the Christian vision which claims that the deepest meaning in life is found in loving God in and through our neighbours, especially the sick, the poor and the marginalised. This is why schools with clear spiritual and philosophical visions have become so important in our time, both for religious people and those of secular conviction. All schools need to be clear, not only on their vision of the human person, but also on how this vision counters or coincides with the dominant images of human transformation offered by the wider social and cultural life of the nation. Children need to be equipped to read the signs of the times and to discern the strengths and weaknesses of the cultural environment in which they live.

Education: negotiating values

Before we compare Catholic schools with schools which espouse a secular philosophy of education, two points must be made regarding the relationship between philosophies of education and actual educational practice in schools. First, education is never a neutral activity. All human knowing involves belief and interpretation. Everyone comes to the task of education with certain prejudices, biases, assumptions and beliefs. Unfortunately, even though the modern 'myth of neutrality' has been thoroughly critiqued by the social, natural and humanistic sciences, many people continue to consider it to be common sense.[12] Nevertheless, it is important to insist that there is nothing neutral or value-free about any system of schooling, secular or faith-based; they each propose a certain vision of reality and of human life as the most true or real. As Brenda Watson notes:

> Whereas religion openly affirms and celebrates, thus making itself vulnerable to the charge of confessionalism, secularists argue that they are not instilling any belief about God, but just allowing people to think what they want; by not teaching about God it is presumed that a tolerant, neutral, flat playing-field is achieved. Secularism, however, is not neutral in its understanding of reality. It rests on the belief that there is no God and that the world can be adequately – as fully explained as is possible or necessary - in wholly molecular terms. The fact that secularists are normally reluctant to admit that they operate from a faith basis enables the myth of their neutrality to continue flourishing.[13]

When comparing educational philosophies it is also important to remember that a stated commitment to particular educational principles and values is no guarantee that they are pursued in practice. There is great variation in the degree to which the whole ethos of the school mirrors the ideals that are aspired to by the patron body or the educational tradition being drawn upon. This is true because of the cultural complexities mentioned above; the obligation on schools to implement the State's educational policies for schools; parental aspirations for children's schooling related to social class; and a disconnection between the rhetoric of those charged with championing a particular schooling type and the extent to which teachers, managers and principals on the ground actually share the aspirations, values and commitments espoused by organisations or institutions at a public level.[14] There is also a sense in which all structured educational experiences are living conversations which are continually renewed and developed as new generations of teachers bring their own experience to bear upon them.[15] This characterises education as belonging to a living tradition to which no one agency has an unequivocal claim. Thus one would expect to find local variation in the school policies (e.g. discipline, pupil and teacher appraisal, social justice, intercultural, educational disadvantage, anti-racism, enrolment), styles of leadership, pupil-teacher interactions, and pedagogical approaches implemented in schools which share a common patronage model, because of varying levels of understanding and commitment by teachers to the philosophy of education espoused by the patrons. Educational traditions are by their nature dialogical even if certain conversations are understandably given priority.

What Irish primary schools have in common

It is important to appreciate the values and commitments that are shared by Irish primary schools of different patronage. All schools in the Irish State assume a framework of values consistent with a concern for democracy, social justice and human rights as they all seek to form students who will be good citizens in a pluralist democratic society.[16] In this context it is understood that all schools will educate children into appropriate forms of freedom and autonomy. In practice this means that young children will be encouraged to adopt the ideas, attitudes and actions of key adults around them such that they develop a secure basis for development. Then, as they grow older, children will be empowered to decide autonomously whether to adopt beliefs, attitudes or values that they have hitherto accepted on authority, whether in denominational, non-denominational or multi-denominational schools.[17]

Schools in a liberal democracy share the values of equality, tolerance, and responsibility, even though the way in which these values are understood, and the relative importance given to such values, might differ. So while children in all schools will be taught the values of tolerance and respect, for example, a Catholic school will enjoin students to go beyond mere tolerance to self-giving love of others (*agápē*) – a hospitable approach to the other which is supported by deep religious beliefs about their sacred dignity as created by God.

All Irish primary schools will seek to develop some sense of community in the school, in the sense of a group of people dedicated to implementing a shared vision of education. Most schools will aim to be inclusive, respectfully accommodating the actual diversity of religion and beliefs present within their educational communities, while upholding their own particular ethos and identity, whether denominational, multi-denominational or non-denominational. Finally, each type of school will include within their community teachers and pupils of other religious and non-religious traditions and so all Irish primary schools are properly described as 'multi-religious; multi-faith/multi-world view'.[18]

The Primary School Curriculum (1999) is implemented in all primary schools. Therefore all teachers are expected to employ child-centred approaches and aim to foster rational freedom, creativity and active learning. Similarly, the approach to religious or ethical education taken by all schools will have certain characteristics in common. The religious freedom of children will be respected and religions and worldviews will be presented fairly and accurately in the religious or ethical education programmes of all schools. Table 1 provides an overview of the commitments that should be shared by all primary schools.

Table 1: Commitments shared by all Primary Schools
- Care for the child
- Fostering respect for the dignity of the person
- Commitment and integrity
- Valuing of diversity
- Sharing values such as solidarity, tolerance, freedom and inclusivity
- Respecting people of all religious beliefs and other stances for living
- Teaching children to take responsibility for their judgements and beliefs
- Laying foundations for autonomy
- Forming children for responsible and active citizenship
- Stewardship and care of the environment
- Commitment to children's moral and spiritual development
- Supporting democracy and equality under the law
- Respect for human rights, freedom of conscience and of religion
- Promoting justice and peace

- Recognising and supporting the pivotal role played by parents and guardians in the formation of their children's stance for living
- Serving national development
- The ethical/religious education curriculum is integrated (where appropriate) with other curriculum subjects

Schools are distinctive

Summarising the literature on values in education, Carmel Mulcahy proposes that schools are 'the repositories of a set of core values which can be transmitted to students'.[19] While the process by which values cherished by adults are passed on to the next generation is extremely complex, schools (along with parents, community leaders and other children) continue to commit themselves to forming children in the values they think will best enable children to live good lives in the present and as a basis for growth in adulthood. While Irish primary schools share many of the same values and commitments, they differ significantly in the emphasis placed on certain values relating to the understanding of reality and of the human person and the purposes of education proposed by the school.

Because values (and their underpinning beliefs) inevitably conflict, schools decide, day in day out, which values actually have overriding importance. The priority given to certain values in a school gives a clue to the distinctive kind of vision of human development being proposed by that school.[20] For example, a secular school might highlight the liberal values of autonomy, children's rights and equity, while a Catholic school might emphasise religious values such as belonging in community, dependence on and gratitude to God, forgiveness and love of others.

Educate Together schools

Educate Together schools are multi-denominational schools which espouse an explicitly secular ethos.[21] This means that the foundational beliefs, principles and values on which these schools operate aim to relate children to the natural order of space and time, and that the scientific paradigm is assumed as the default model for understanding life and creation. The basic philosophy underpinning the schools' approach to education could be described as worldly or immanent, as opposed to a Catholic philosophy of education which includes a transcendent dimension. As religious sources have no impact on the philosophy of education proposed by Educate Together schools, religious communities have no right of membership on the Board of Management, and religious instruction does not occur during the school day. Religion is seen as a private matter for the individual, though a child's right to practise a religion is respected.

Educate Together schools draw on a secular liberal philosophy of education.[22] Principles and values typical of liberal education include personal autonomy, rationality, equality of respect, development of multicultural education and an emphasis on education for citizenship, human rights and democracy.[23] In general, because priority cannot be given to any worldview beyond the secular, these schools tend to aim to actively promote the values of basic social morality and 'civic' or democratic skills and virtues more generally.[24] Children are formed in ethical dispositions and skills necessary for participating in a liberal democratic society. Here, moral education is clearly distinguished from religious education. Moral education is a secular enterprise which appeals to secular norms of reason that govern behaviour.

According to Carmel Mulcahy, Educate Together schools aim to 'foster an understanding of values' which are 'relevant in preparing students to play an informed, but caring role, as citizens in an increasingly pluralist world'. Each Educate Together school presents 'an overall system of values' which coincides to varying degrees with the value frameworks of children in the school.[25] This system of values often finds expression in a 'core curriculum' or an 'ethical curriculum' which is understood to replace the traditional religious education curriculum for these schools. Ideally, the values in the ethical curriculum are negotiated between teachers, parents and guardians according to democratic principles. One would expect to find some differences therefore in the actual values and perspectives prioritised in any particular Educate Together school.[26]

Many Educate Together schools use the *Learn Together Ethical Curriculum*. This ethical curriculum is described by Mulcahy as 'the formal method of fostering pluralist values in students'.[27] Here ethics are taught while prescinding from the religious identities and formation of children. The curriculum takes an approach to ethical education which emphasises questions of equality, justice, sustainability and active citizenship. There is a strong emphasis on the development of critical awareness, moral decision-making skills, 'inner discovery', critical examination of values and on individual empowerment.

One strand of the *Learn Together* curriculum is the 'Belief Systems' strand. The aim of this strand is to promote a 'pluralist approach' to religions and beliefs in students. This means that children are taught to affirm and celebrate a plurality of religious and non-religious stances for living.[28] Here it is assumed that, as children have different religious and spiritual identities, they should be invited to explore these while 'being aware of and respecting the notion that other people may think differently to them'.[29] The basic philosophical assumption for this exploration is that all cultures are worthwhile and valuable and that no single perspective on reality or the person is truer than any other. By affirming that all worldviews are equal, and that judgements between worldviews is socially inappropriate, it is hoped to foster a positive attitude toward religions and other stances for living in general. In sum, the political principles of liberal democracy underpin the pedagogical approach to religion adopted here.

Catholic schools

The philosophy of Catholic schools is based on a Christian view of life, and educational values in Catholic schools are negotiated within an explicit horizon of faith. Christian faith offers a strong, radically hopeful message regarding human life and its ultimate meaning. Here it is acknowledged that there is a transcendent dimension to life and that life is best lived within the context of love and worship of God. In sum, God (understood as ultimate truth, goodness, beauty) is seen as the ultimate foundation of education in a Catholic school.

The word 'Catholic' means an explicit concern for the whole, for all creation, and the common good. This peculiarly Catholic way of proceeding has been summarised by Charles Taylor as a search for 'universality through wholeness'.[30] As a religion that seeks out the broadest scope of God's gracious action and presence in the world, Catholic Christianity approaches pluralism as an invitation to dialogue. In other words, Catholics will be concerned with the difference that difference makes. They will desire not only to seek the meaning of difference but will seek for the unity across difference wherever it can be found. In line with this conviction, Catholic schools strive to be inclusive in welcoming children of all religious faiths and worldviews.

The Catholic school proposes that education is about learning how to relate in ever more true ways to the presence of God in oneself, in other people, and in the created world. Because God is an intimate part of our very selves, no part of the person's development and hence no part of his or her education could be outside the sphere of God's love and attention. For the Catholic it would be impossible to consider educating children apart from their life in God. The Catholic school offers a distinctive vision of transformation to that offered by secular schools, because here it is assumed that it is God who does the transforming, in tandem with us, always respecting our freedom and autonomy, but inviting us to live a life of love and responsibility.

In the Catholic school, ethics are taught in the context of the religious formation of the person as it is believed that ethics cannot be separated out from the person's religious life. Therefore, religious education has an essential role in the moral education of students. Catholic moral education is sustained by the Christian narrative that provides ideals and a sense of meaning, purpose and hope. This narrative is offered to children as a source of illumination and motivation for their lives. So, for example, while Catholic schools will share a commitment to social justice with other schools, this commitment is based on a vision of justice and social transformation that goes beyond human effort and rests on God's promise of justice for the victims of history.

The Catholic school emphasises training in virtue (as opposed to value formation), that is, in nurturing certain ways of acting with respect to self, others, the created world and God. For example, the Catholic school will prioritise the virtue of love, since for Christians the essence of a good life is a life lived in love of self, others, creation and God. Pupils are also taught the virtue of gratitude – not to take the gifts of life for granted, and to acknowledge their dependence on others and on God. As Louis Dupré explains:

> In gratitude we temporarily abandon the standpoint of our own private needs and affirm our dependence with respect to the other. In this attitude of profound humility we cease to take ourselves as the centre of existence ... Yet gratitude does not consist in passive resignation; it actively reaches out to the other, regardless of personal feelings or desires. As such it sets the primary condition for any kind of spiritual life and, indeed, for Christian love itself. For to love in the Christian sense I must first forsake my private, possessive love of the creature and take it on its own terms, love it for its own sake.[31]

Table 2 summarises some differences in the philosophical perspectives, commitments and values espoused by Catholic schools (Table 2.1) and Educate Together schools (Table 2.2). It is offered as a guide for students and practising teachers to prompt discussion and reflection on the different educational narratives, ideological visions and communities of meaning offered by the two types of school.

Table 2.1 The Philosophy of Education of *Catholic Schools*

Commitments (values, virtues, emphases)	Understanding of the person, human flourishing and human destiny	Understanding of Life/Reality Worldview	Purpose/goal of schooling
In the intellectual realm, wisdom and contemplation are the highest values. Distinctiveness, openness and inclusiveness (*Kata-holos* – welcoming everybody). Openness to the will of God. Forgiveness, compassion and mercy. Inter-dependence and responsibility to self and others. Love of neighbour.	Taken from theology and philosophy; person created in God's image and called to life in Christ through the Holy Spirit. Person is a union of body and soul. The unique dignity of the person is grounded in their dependence on, and a participation in, God. Every person's religious, spiritual, cultural, ethnic identity is respected.	Assumes that there is a supernatural or transcendent reality as well as the natural universe of space and time. Life is affirmed within a transcendent horizon. God is the foundation of all reality and the deepest meaning of everything created (myself, other people, creation).	Integral Formation: development of all human abilities: intellectual, Physical, Emotional, Aesthetic, Spiritual/ Religious; Education for 'wholeness' includes a transcendent dimension. Development and discipline of all the powers of body and soul. Inculcating sense of the ultimate purpose of life and of moral norms for life (in God).

Commitments (values, virtues, emphases)	Understanding of the person, human flourishing and human destiny	Understanding of Life/Reality Worldview	Purpose/goal of schooling
Self-sacrifice. Memory (value of tradition) and hope (the promise of God's future). 'Autonomy via faith'.[32] Acceptance of religious authority in the service of freedom.[33] Preferential option for the poor. Offering prophetic witness to the world. Welcoming the stranger.	Human flourishing is enhanced by responding to Revelation and the authority of religious tradition. God grants children freedom to work out the meaning of their lives in responsibility to God's presence in self, others and creation. Recognition of sin and failure as part of life, the need for forgiveness, the mercy and compassion of a God who heals. Emphasis on person-in-community.	God has revealed Godself and I can come to know God. Accepts religious authority of Scripture and Tradition: Faith *and* Reason help me come to know what is true.	Discovering gift of personal freedom Education for citizenship in a democratic society, for membership of the Church and as citizens of the world to come. Fostering openness, creativity, imagination, sacramental consciousness, perception of beauty, deeper sense of language, joy, capacity for wonder, sense of justice, compassion. Education for dialogue with those of other faiths, social justice, stewardship of creation.

Table 2.2 The Philosophy of Education of *Educate Together Schools*

Commitments (values, virtues, emphases)[34]	Understanding of the person, human flourishing and human destiny	Understanding of Life/Reality Worldview	Purpose/goal of schooling
In the intellectual realm, rational autonomy is the highest value. Liberal values: individual liberty and freedom of conscience, equality of respect for all individuals, consistent rationality, principles of impartiality and tolerance, personal autonomy.	Taken from social science and liberal philosophy. Children understood as independent individuals and as citizens. Identity understood in terms of individual autonomy. Dignity of the self emerges from the autonomy of the self. Children's social, cultural and religious identities are acknowledged, respected and celebrated.	Based on the natural universe of space and time. Life is affirmed within an immanent horizon. Does not make any commitment on either the nature of truth or metaphysical reality or spirituality, or the existence of non-physical entities such as God, souls or angels.	Development of the person and the powers of human nature (intellectual, physical, emotional, spiritual and moral). Education for 'wholeness', excludes a transcendent dimension. Development of rational autonomy and critical openness and civic mindedness. Preparation for life in a liberal democratic society: work, democracy, citizenship, participation, harmonious co-existence with others, racial equality, social integration.

Commitments (values, virtues, emphases)	Understanding of the person, human flourishing and human destiny	Understanding of Life/Reality Worldview	Purpose/goal of schooling
Other sample values: Social justice, Inclusiveness, Self-esteem, Valuing self, Self-motivation, Individuality/ Independence, Human dignity, Self-knowledge, Confidence, Honesty/ trustworthiness, Equity, Openness, Freedom, Mutual understanding, Civic mindedness, Respect for environment. Commitment to human rights and global justice. 'Autonomy via reason'.[35]	Children are understood without reference to anything that transcends them; the self is an absolute centre in its own right. The self is the primary source of meaning. Human flourishing is enhanced when I am able to assert and respond to rights grounded in an autonomous rationality that is universally accessible. No particular reference point for the destiny of human beings after death.	Human autonomy Is valued over religious authority; I come to know what is true using my human powers of rationality.	Focus on public or civic moral formation, e.g. education for human rights advocacy and/or activism. Developing rational thinking and autonomous judgement as sources of civic behaviour and public moral conduct. Multi-cultural education. Citizenship education. Democratic education. Human rights education. Global justice education. Education in the values in the first column.

Conclusion

Education enables children to search for a meaningful *spirituality* or *philosophy of life* in the context of particular traditions of thought and living. Different schooling types are based on shared narratives that give a sense of purpose and distinguish them from other schools. Each school invites students to explore some ideal, some image of full human development, suggesting a coherent moral framework and a shared horizon of meaning for their lives, a horizon based on either secular values, transcendent values or both. While Catholic schools share much in common with other schools in Irish society, the philosophy of education they propose offers a unique perspective on the purposes of education and the ways in which students are educated in the intellectual, spiritual, moral and religious domains. A genuinely pluralist democracy should be able to accommodate both faith-based and secular philosophies of education, provided that both secular and faith-based schools assume a framework of values consistent with a concern for intellectual, moral and spiritual liberty, democracy, social justice and human rights.

Questions for reflection

» What images of the human are offered as goals to children today in popular culture?

» What is your vision of the human? What would you consider to be a good/false spirituality? Is the human person matter or spirit or both or neither? Where is the ultimate purpose of life to be found?

» Examining a schooling type of your choice, examine the underlying philosophy of education that informs the work of the school:

» a) What truths or ideas concerning the human person are assumed? What aspects of being human are included in the vision? What elements are left out in your view? What makes us more human in this view?

» b) What does the school suggest to children life is about? What does it suggest they might hope for? What vision does that school offer that might help them develop meaning and purpose for their lives? What does it say to them about human failure and suffering?

» c) What is the purpose of education according to this model? What attitudes, dispositions and practices are proposed by which the aims of the school can be pursued?

» Discuss the following statement: 'It is easy to outline a wonderful set of inclusive, progressive values in the school brochure, but a lot more difficult to realise those ideas in practice'. *Mary McAleese, former president of Ireland*[36]

» How do we avoid the current deadlock between charges of indoctrination (levelled against faith-based schools) on the one hand, and charges of 'non-neutrality' (levelled against secular schools) on the other?

Supplementary reading

» Donal Murray, *A Special Concern: The Philosophy of Education: a Christian Perspective* (Dublin: Veritas, 1991).

» The umbrella body representing Catholic Education at a national level is the Catholic Schools Partnership. http://www.catholicshools.ie.

» The Report on the Forum on Patronage and Pluralism in the Primary Sector (2012) is available on the website of the Department of Education and Skills, found at www.education.ie.

» David Tuohy, *Denominational Education and Politics* (Dublin: Veritas, 2013). Explores issues of pluralism, diversity and rights in the context of Europe. The Forum on Patronage and Pluralism is discussed here.

» Caroline Renehan, *Openness with Roots: Education in Religion in Irish Primary Schools* (Newcastle upon Tyne: Cambridge Scholars Publishing, 2014). Considers the historical legacy and current debate concerning religious education in the Republic of Ireland.

» Gareth Byrne and Patricia Kieran (eds), *Toward Mutual Ground: Pluralism, Religious Education and Diversity In Irish Schools* (Dublin: Columba Press, 2013). A good overview of the present debate in Ireland on the challenges posed by the existence of social and religious pluralism in Irish schools.

» Micheál Mac Gréil, *Pluralism and Diversity in Ireland: Prejudice and Related Issues in Early 21st Century Ireland* (Dublin: Columba Press, 2011).

On faith schools

» J. Mark Halstead, 'Faith Schools' in L. Philip Barnes (ed.), *Debates in Religious Education* (London: Routledge, 2012), 103–7.

» J. Mark Halstead, 'In Defence of Faith Schools' in Graham Haydon (ed.), *Faith in Education: a Tribute to Terence McLaughlin* (London: Institute of Education, University of London, 2009), 46–67.

» Liam Gearon, *MasterClass in Religious Education: Transforming Teaching and Learning* (London: Bloomsbury, 2013), Chapter 3.

» John Sullivan, 'Faith Schools: a Culture within a Culture in a Changing World' in Marian de Souza et al. (eds),

International Handbook of the Religious, Moral and Spiritual Dimensions in Education (Dordrecht: Springer, 2006), 937–47.

» Hanan A. Alexander and Ayman K. Agabaria, *Commitment, Character, and Citizenship: Religious Education in Liberal Democracy* (New York, NY: Routledge, 2012), on the issue of how faith-based schools contribute to a student's ability to participate effectively in a liberal democratic society (particularly the articles of Walter Feinberg and Steven C. Vryhof). On the potential contribution of faith schools to citizenship in a liberal democratic society, see James C. Conroy's essay in the same volume.

Endnotes

1. Steven C. Vryhof, 'Between Memory and Vision: Schools as Communities of Meaning', in Hanan A. Alexander and Ayman K. Agbaria (eds), *Commitment, Character, and Citizenship: Religious Education in Liberal Democracy* (London: Routledge, 2012), 47.
2. G. K. Chesterton, *The Common Man* (London: Sheed and Ward, 1950), 167–8.
3. Andrew Wright, 'The justification of compulsory religious education: a response to Professor White', *British Journal of Religious Education* (2004), 26(2): 168.
4. For discussion of the way in which all education, particularly that of small children, contains a strongly formative element, see Elmer John Thiessen, *Teaching For Commitment: Liberal Education, Indoctrination and Christian Nurture* (Leominster: Gracewing, 1993), 92–8.
5. John L. Elias, 'Ancient Philosophy and Religious Education: education as initiation into a way of life' in M. de Souza et al. (eds), *International Handbook of the Religious, Moral and Spiritual Dimensions in Education* (Dordrecht: Springer, 2006), 12. See also Steven C. Vryhof on the importance of schooling offering communities of meaning which pass on a 'cultural memory' and offer a 'cultural vision' to children. Steven C. Vryhof, 'Between Memory and Vision: Schools as Communities of Meaning' in Hanan A. Alexander and Ayman K. Agbaria (eds), *Commitment, Character, and Citizenship: Religious Education in a Liberal Democracy* (London: Routledge, 2012), 46–59.
6. Pádraig Hogan, 'Teaching and Learning as a Way of Life', *Journal of Philosophy of Education* (2003), 37(2): 216; Peter Redpath, 'foreword' to Curtis L. Hancock, *Recovering a Catholic Philosophy of Elementary Education* (Mount Pocono, PA: Newman House Press, 2005), 13.
7. Hogan, 'Teaching and Learning as a Way of Life', 215.
8. On the way in which schools offer different conceptions of 'wholeness' in education see Andrew O' Shea, 'Education for wholeness in an age of global citizenship: staying with the problem of value(s)', *Irish Educational Studies* (2013), 32(3): 275–89.
9. Anne Hunt, 'The Essence of Education is Religious', in M. de Souza et al. (eds), ibid., 647.
10. Michael Warren, 'Religious Formation in the Context of Social Formation', in Jeff Astley and Leslie Francis (eds), *Critical Perspectives on Christian Education*, (Leominster, Herefordshire: Gracewing, Fowler Wright Books, 1994), 206–7.
11. Warren, 'Religious Formation', pp. 208–9.
12. For a more detailed exploration of this point, see Dermot A. Lane, *Religion and Education: Re-imagining the Relationship* (Dublin: Veritas, 2013), 41–2, and Gavin D'Costa, 'Catholicism, Religious Pluralism and Education for the Common Good' in Gareth Byrne and Patricia Kieran (eds), *Toward Mutual Ground: Pluralism, Religious Education and Diversity in Irish Schools* (Dublin: Columba Press, 2012), 115.
13. Brenda Watson, 'Secularism, schools and religious education' in Marius Felderhof, Penny Thompson and David Torevell (eds), *Inspiring Faith in Schools* (Hampshire: Ashgate, 2007), 8.
14. Recent research published by the Economic and Social Research Institute (ESRI) into the Irish schooling system at primary and secondary levels reveals that the choice of schools is far more complex than simply being based upon parents' espousal of religious or secular belief. See M. Darmody and E. Smyth,

'Governance and funding of voluntary secondary schools in Ireland', Dublin: ESRI, 2013, and M. Darmody, E. Smyth and S. McCoy, 'School Sector variation among primary schools in Ireland' (Dublin: ESRI, 2012). Both reports are available on the ESRI website, http://www.esri.ie.

15. Jones Irwin draws attention to significant intra-Catholic diversity in educational philosophy in Jones Irwin, 'Toward Change: Exploring Tensions in Ethical-Religious Pedagogy in Irish Primary Education' in Kieran and Byrne (eds), ibid., 179–80. On significantly different approaches to the inclusion of non-Catholic students in Catholic schools, see Maurice Ryan, 'Including students who are not Catholics in Catholic schools: problems, issues and responses' in Stephen McKinney (ed.), *Faith Schools in the Twenty-First Century* (Edinburgh: Dunedin Academic Press, 2008), 30–40.

16. On the new framework which is evolving for the consideration of the role and nature of religious education in the 'public space' based upon the work of various United Nations agencies concerning the definition and promotion of human rights, see Andrew McGrady, 'Religious Education, Citizenship and Human Rights: Perspectives from the United Nations and the Council of Europe', in M. de Souza et al. (eds), Ibid., 977–992.

17. On the idea of teaching children for 'autonomy-via-faith', see T. H. McLaughlin, 'Parental rights and the religious upbringing of children', *Journal of Philosophy of Education* (1984) 18 (1): 75–83. Hanan Alexander proposes that the alternative option — schools which propose that reason and not religion should determine life choices, be called 'autonomy-via-reason'. Hanan A. Alexander, 'Autonomy, faith and reason: McLaughlin and Callan on religious initiation' in Graham Haydon (ed), *Faith in Education: a tribute to Terence McLaughlin* (London: Institute of Education, University of London, 2009), 29.

18. McGrady, 'Teaching Religion' in Byrne and Kieran (eds), ibid., 89.

19. Carmel Mulcahy, 'Values in Education: A Pluralist Perspective' in Catherine Furlong and Luke Monahan (eds), *School Culture and Ethos: Cracking the Code* (Dublin: Marino Institute of Education, 2000), 84.

20. Another clue is to be found in the dominant discourses which inform the curriculum in any particular school, e.g. particular discourses of multiculturalism, human rights and citizenship, particular understandings of integral formation, spiritual wholeness, well-being, social justice, etc.

21. Multi-denominational is a contested term which is currently used by schools under the patronage or trusteeship of non-religious bodies such as the local Education and Training Boards (formerly VEC) or Educate Together. These schools differ in the extent to which religious bodies have any involvement in the running of the school. In some schools (e.g. Community National Schools), members of religious communities have a right to sit on a Board of Management and these schools provide for religious instruction during the school day. In other schools (e.g. Educate Together), there is a more explicitly secular ethos, religious communities have no right of membership on the Board of Management, and religious instruction does not occur during the school day. For a suggested use of the terms 'multi-denominational' and non-denominational, see McGrady, 'Teaching Religion' in Byrne and Kieran (eds), ibid., 86–77 (McGrady's definitions are used in the glossary of this book).

22. This vision is set out in *The Educate Together Charter* (2004) found at http: // www.educatetogether.ie/about-2/-charter/ and *What is an Educate Together School?* (Dublin: Educate Together, 2005).

23. J. M. Halstead, 'Liberal Values and Liberal Education' in Wilfred Carr (ed.), *The Routledge Falmer Reader in Philosophy of Education* (London: Routledge, 2005), 115–18.

24. Terence H. McLaughlin, 'Liberalism, Education and the Common School', *Journal of Philosophy of Education* (1995), 29(2): 241.

25. Mulcahy, ibid., 93.

26. One Educate Together school studied by Anne Marie Kavanagh in her research was found to favour a multicultural education model and 'a rights based approach to education'. In this school practices and policies in the school are informed by a particular discourse of multicultural education and are designed to support social justice, participation in the democratic process, civic responsibility, anti-racism and structural equity for teachers and students. Here emphasis is placed on increasing students' familiarity with and understanding of social justice through the lens of multicultural discourse, on forming children as human rights advocates and on active citizenship. Anne Marie Kavanagh, 'Emerging Models of Intercultural Education in Irish Primary Schools: A Critical Case Study Analysis', PhD thesis, 2013, St. Patrick's College, Dublin City University, Unpublished. Kavanagh's research highlights the significant impact individual principals have on the distinctive ethos and philosophy of particular Educate Together schools.

27. Mulcahy, ibid., 91.

28. The Belief Systems strand seems to be underpinned by commitments common to liberal models of religious education. However, the authors have not outlined the philosophical principles underpinning the strand so comments made here are very tentative. The approach to religions which are conceptualised as 'cultural ways of life' seems to stem from liberal multicultural theory. On what she terms 'benevolent forms of multicultural education', see Ann Marie Kavanagh, ibid., 141

29. Mary Kelleher et al., *Learn Together: An Ethical Education Curriculum for Educate Together Schools* (Dublin: Educate Together, 2004), 9.

30. James L. Heft (ed.), *A Catholic Modernity? Charles Taylor's Marianist Award Lecture* (New York: Oxford University Press, 1999), 14.

31. Louis Dupré, 'Catholic Education and the Predicament of Modern Culture', *The Living Light* (1987), 23 (4): 305.

32. T. H. McLaughlin, 'Parental rights and the religious upbringing of children' in *Journal of Philosophy of Education* (1984), 18(1): 79.

33. Richard McBrien, *Catholicism*, vol. II (Geoffrey Chapman: London, 1980), 1174.

34. The core liberal values and principles are taken from Halstead 'Liberal Values and Liberal Education', 111-112. Other sample values have been taken from the 'core values' found by Carmel Mulcahy in her research in a number of *Educate Together* Schools. See Mulcahy, Ibid, 83-95.

35. See note 17 above.

36. Mary McAleese, 'The School as a Partnership of Care', Introduction to Furlong and Monahan (eds), Ibid., xiii

CHAPTER TWO
CATHOLIC EDUCATION: A THEOLOGICAL PERSPECTIVE

Honouring particularity is not opposed to valuing pluralism; indeed the former is a necessary pre-condition for the existence of the latter.[1]

FAYETTE BREAUX VEVERKA

... [O]ne might consider it one of the main objectives of the Catholic school. To *de-religionize* our faith by extending the religious attitude beyond the limits of sacred doctrine to all areas of existence.[2]

LOUIS DUPRÉ

I have come that you may have life and have it to the full.

(JN 10:10)

ONE DAY AT THE BEGINNING OF A LECTURE, A STUDENT TEACHER ASKED me the question: why would I want to teach in a Catholic school? I answered her as follows: you should consider teaching in a Catholic school if the foundational principles, values and ideals of Catholic education appeal to you. Most importantly, the Catholic vision of education must make sense to you in your own life, in light of your own questions, experiences, struggles and your developing understanding of the human journey. This will depend on things like whether working in an environment where the presence of God is assumed matters to you or not; whether you find the Catholic view of the person and of what constitutes 'personal development' to be truer than alternative accounts of the meaning and purpose of human life; whether you consider that the person of Jesus Christ and the way he lived adds anything unique to your understanding and experience of the human journey; whether you are open to viewing your teaching career simply as a profession or as a vocation – as part of the Church's work in the world.

This chapter proposes a theological vision for Catholic schools. A Catholic school is described as a school which offers a holistic view of education, celebrates God's reign, places relationship with Jesus Christ at the centre, and builds a community serving the mission of the Church in the world. Some of the practical implications of this vision are explored with a view to helping teachers to discern how Catholic education can maintain its distinctiveness in a pluralist educational environment. In practice, of course, each Catholic school will draw up its own mission statement outlining the principles, values and ideals which it wishes to see embodied through its curriculum and ethos. These will reflect the historical traditions of the school, the contemporary cultural setting and make-up of the school (in terms of pupils and teachers), the guidelines on Catholic schools issued by the Irish Episcopal Conference, together with contemporary scholarship on Catholic education, on Catholic theology and on a Catholic philosophy of education generally. As a result one would expect to find a variety of models of Catholic school, which meet the needs and priorities of people in different areas of Ireland. Nevertheless, a focus on what Catholic schools might have in common is necessary at a time when Irish Catholic primary education is challenged by educational philosophies and approaches that are sometimes at odds with a Catholic philosophy of education.

The starting place: God

The Catholic school is a faith-based school. This means that its *raison-d'être* begins with God. Catholics believe that God created the world and that the ultimate destiny of the world and of each and every person is *in* God. The amazing 'good news' that Christianity proposes is this: God is present within each person, inviting all of us to be in loving relationship with him. In other words, each and every person is invited to respond to the fact that they already share God's life. God has created us simply because God wants to be in a relationship with people who can respond.

The theologian Michael Himes has suggested that, for Christians, God can best be understood using the metaphor of self-giving love. The first epistle of John states this truth clearly: 'God is love' (1 Jn 4: 8). This belief in a relational God of love, says Himes, is 'the deepest claim that Christianity offers about the Mystery that undergirds our existence'.[3] To claim that God is love makes a profound difference to how

Christians understand themselves, their students, their colleagues and the whole profession of teaching. This is because, for Christians, love is the foundation of everything that exists. This means that if we are to really appreciate *anything* in its depth, we must see that it is held in existence by the love of God for it. This powerful claim is called *sacramentality*. It means that any person, place, or thing – anything that exists – can be sacramental if one appreciates that it is rooted in the presence and love of God.[4]

This distinctive claim about reality and about human persons is central to the vision of education proposed by Catholic schools. It means first of all that Catholic educators will seek to help their students become attuned to the presence of God in everything: in themselves, in their work, in everyone they meet and in the whole created world. God will be referred to regularly during the everyday work of the school and children will be helped to relate their normal experiences of work and play to the presence of God in their midst. Further, Catholic teachers will aim to foster the habit of attention, wonder, imagination and a search for truth in their students. They will assume that the universe has a God-given purpose and design and that all of creation is vivified by the Creator Spirit. Finally, an experience of joy, gratitude and dependence on God will be developed and sustained through the power of liturgy and prayer in the Catholic school.

A Catholic sacramental perspective on curriculum suggests the importance of not creating too sharp a distinction between the religious curriculum and other subjects on the curriculum, while at the same time respecting the autonomy of every subject.[5] While every subject taught in the Catholic school has its own integrity and must be taught according to its own particular principles and methods,[6] when viewed from a sacramental perspective every subject in the Catholic school will be understood as holy in its depths. So, for example, during a science class, children might be encouraged to wonder at the marvels of God's creation and to appreciate God's intimate care for every organism on the planet. They might also be invited to examine the value of scientific skills and progress from a Christian ethical perspective. There is a world of difference between the use of scientific skill to create bombs and the use of such skill to find a cure for cancer, for example. On this understanding, religious education in the Catholic school will never be seen as an appendage onto an otherwise profane curriculum; instead, religious education will be understood as the core curriculum subject as it draws children's attention to the fact that everything and everyone is grounded in the love of God.

God and the child

A Catholic perspective on education understands children primarily in terms of their relationship to God. The child is seen as a person created in God's image and called to life in Christ through the Holy Spirit. Each person is understood as a spiritual being who was created by God and whose destiny is to be with God when this life is over. Because the person is a union of body and soul, the child is understood to have an innate capacity or natural potential for relationship with God. In other words, the child is seen as essentially or intrinsically religious.[7] Pope Benedict XVI described this 'religious dimension of the person' as '... an integral part of the person from the very earliest infancy: it is fundamental openness to otherness and to the mystery that presides over every relationship and every encounter with human beings'.[8] Catholic teachers will see it as their primary duty to help children to appreciate their spiritual depth, theological mystery, and moral dignity. Children will be invited to understand themselves as having both a physical and spiritual nature, and they will be invited to cultivate in themselves 'an inner life as the place to listen to the voice of God'.[9]

Children in Catholic schools will always be reminded that they are created in the image and likeness of God and that as such they are essentially *good*.[10] With this in mind, Catholic teachers will take a basically compassionate and forgiving approach to students, believing the best of them, giving them a second chance, and going the 'extra mile' to ensure they reach their fullest potential, whatever their circumstances. When children experience the love of God for them as well as their identity as children of God, it forms the basis for healthy development of Christian moral character and ethical living in the world.

Catholics understand that human beings are not isolated individuals but persons who are essentially relational and social. Every human being is called to communion because they have been created in the image and likeness of the communion of love of the three persons of the Trinity. Therefore, we become persons only in and through our relationships with others, and the meaning of our existence lies, not in serving our own ends, but in the call to 'the duty to exist for others'.[11] Children in Catholic schools will be invited to see themselves as having an ethical call to serve one another. The curriculum will include the learning of 'skills that are related to knowing and knowing how to do things, but also skills that apply to living alongside others and growing as human beings'.[12] In this way children will be invited to consider their lives as a vocation, as a journey to be lived together.[13] They will be taught that happiness and fulfilment are achieved when people use their God-given gifts and talents for the good of all.

Finally, Catholics believe that human beings are estranged from God, that by 'origin' we are 'prone to sin' and that therefore we have a need for God's mercy and redemption. This understanding has two implications. First, it means that we need God's help in attaining truth and seeking the good in life. The authority of God's revelation is accepted as an integral part of the process by which people come to know what is true and do what is good. Second, our powers of body and soul need discipline as well as development for full human flourishing. In sum, we do not have within ourselves all that is necessary to reach our potential: we need God's guidance and help.[14] In Catholic education, therefore, 'personal development' will never be seen simply as a natural unfolding of the powers or tendencies children bring into the classroom. Instead, their energies and powers of body and soul are to be educated in a way that takes account of their weaknesses as well as their strengths, their capacity for sin, as well as their vocation and capacity – by God's grace – to grow in divine likeness.[15] Children will be helped to recognise that they have potential for development but that there are limits to development, and to appreciate their need for God's help in enabling them to become more loving, responsible and true.

Dignity of the person

The hallmark of the Catholic school is this radical claim: God has been fully expressed in the life, death, and destiny of a particular human being, Jesus of Nazareth. In other words, the Absolute Mystery of God became a fully human being in Jesus. This is called 'the Incarnation'. In his 'Letter to the

Philippians', St. Paul explains that Jesus, 'although he was in the form of God ... did not think being equivalent to God was anything to be held onto, so he emptied himself, taking on the form of a servant and becoming like all other human beings'(Phil 2:6-7). This, Michael Himes reminds us, is the most extraordinary claim of Christian faith because it is a profound statement of the dignity of the human person:

> Notice: the Christian tradition does not say human beings are of such immense dignity that God really loves them. ... No, the Christian tradition says something far more radical: human beings are of such dignity that God has chosen to be one. God does not think being God is anything to be grasped; God empties himself and becomes human like all other human beings. ...

> If one makes this claim of the Incarnation — and it is one whopping great claim to make - then this principle inevitably follows: whatever humanizes, divinizes. That is to say, whatever makes you more genuinely human, more authentically, richly, powerfully human, whatever calls into play all the reaches of your intellect, your freedom, energy, your talents and creativity, makes you more like God. This is how we encounter God in our incarnational tradition: not 'out there' somewhere, but here being human along with us. Whatever makes you more human makes you more like God.[16]

The implication of the Incarnation – of God becoming human – for education is clear: because of the Incarnation, Christian education aims for the fullest possible development of the child in *all* aspects of his or her being: intellectual, moral, spiritual, aesthetic, physical, vocational, social and emotional. Children in Catholic schools will therefore be offered a wealth of opportunities to grow and develop their talents in a wide range of domains. Further, whenever educators in these schools enable and empower children to develop their talents, strengthen their bodies, expand their minds, open their imaginations, and increase their spiritual and aesthetic sensibilities, they will be honouring what unites them with God and supporting them in fulfilling their destiny with God.

Catholic educators will be committed to children's intellectual, physical, spiritual and religious development, in the knowledge that every child's personal development has an intrinsic value regardless of the child's academic ability or potential contribution to the economy or society.[17] Particular attention will be paid to the developmental stage, interests, intellectual, moral and spiritual maturity and cultural background of students in Catholic schools. This is out of respect for the sacredness and human dignity of every person.[18] Rather than assessing their lives primarily in terms of jobs, points, income and prestige, children will be helped to appreciate that real growth consists of developing as a human being and that this is more precious than any wealth: it is what a person *is* rather than what a person *has* that counts.[19] Children will be taught that the ultimate goal of education is to become loving and wise.

A corollary of this idea is that children be enabled to understand that there is more to their lives than their role as citizens. As Donal Murray explains, 'the citizen is, of course, obliged to be loyal and constructive in relation to the State. In the end, however, the State exists for the citizen, not the citizen for the State'.[20] In other words, the life of a person has a meaning beyond that ascribed to her by the society in which she lives. The dignity of the person, created by God and whose ultimate destiny is with God in heaven, is more important than one's social roles.

Finally, in light of their commitment to the sacred dignity of every child, Catholic educators will resist the growing dominance of instrumental reason in education and the perspective which views education as a business enterprise rather than as a public good. Educational practices that are dominated by instrumental or managerial considerations to the detriment of teachers and students have no place in Catholic schools. One such practice is an overemphasis on assessment and performance standards. As John Sullivan has argued, teachers should be encouraged to develop their own teaching style and excessive forms of managerialism or over-dominant leadership should be resisted by teachers in Catholic schools.[21]

Jesus teaches the art of living

The Catholic school proposes that the person of Jesus, the way he lived and his vision of life, is of absolute significance for understanding how to live a good human life. For Christians, Jesus reveals to us true humanity (what it means to be a human being) and true divinity (who God is) and offers us a personal relationship which is salvific.[22] For over two thousand years, Christians have experienced the meaning of their life as transfigured because of the meaning of Jesus' life, death and resurrection. In other words, their ordinary human experiences of working, playing, suffering, celebrating and dying are given an additional, unique and irreplaceable meaning because of the life, death and resurrection of Jesus.

The proclamation of the Kingdom of God was at the heart of Jesus' work. In the gospels of Mark and Matthew we read, 'Jesus came to Galilee, proclaiming the good news from God', and saying, 'the time is fulfilled and the Kingdom of God has come near; repent, and believe in the good news' (Mk 1: 14–15; Mt 4: 17). Describing the Kingdom (Reign) of God, Pope Benedict XVI explains:

> The Kingdom of God is not a thing, a social or political structure, a utopia. ... Kingdom of God means: God exists, God is alive. God is present and acts in the world, in our – in my life. God is not a faraway 'ultimate cause', God is not the 'great architect' of deism, who created the machine of the world and is no longer part of it – on the contrary: God is the most present and decisive reality in each and every act of my life, in each and every moment of history.[23]

Jesus emerged as the one who, more than any other person in history, lived as though God was the most present and decisive reality in each moment and act of his life and as though no one else had any power over him. Rooted in his deep prayer relationship with God, he invited people to live as though God now reigned and shared his imagination of a world beyond legalism, superstition, and fear.[24] Anointed and empowered by the Spirit of God, Jesus devoted his ministry to healing and reconciling, to building up human persons, especially the poor and the downtrodden. His firm belief was that through his ministry God was acting to transform people's lives, thus bringing about healing and salvation.

When Jesus healed social outcasts, such as the ten lepers (Lk 17:11-14), the crippled woman (Lk 13:10-17) or the haemorrhaging woman (Lk 8:43-48), his action was a sign of the presence and salvation of God. Again, through his fellowship meals, Jesus revealed that in the Kingdom of God there are no distinctions and hierarchies between male and female, rich and poor, Gentile and Jew. (Indeed, his followers were mainly made up of those who were excluded and marginalised, including women.) Jesus aroused these people to unconditional faith in God. He told the sinful woman, 'Your faith has saved you; go in peace.' (Lk 7:50), teaching that God's Spirit did not impose itself upon them externally but transformed them from within. The God he knew recreates everything – heart, mind and body – providing the strength for people to transform themselves and their world.[25]

Jesus was even willing to endure suffering and persecution, so that the Kingdom of God might come. Throughout his ministry he endured real, constant and increasing persecution – a suffering which culminated in his horrific death. Yet, even though he was aware of the possibility of being put to death, he deliberately continued his work. Thus, though Jesus died, as a religious–political criminal on a cross, this last action in his life's passion was not only done to him, but something he freely chose.[26] He died because he was faithful to his message to the end.

At the Last Supper Jesus expressed his understanding that his death did not nullify his hope. He expressed his desire that his followers would guarantee the continuity of his life's work. As he brought bread and shared the cup of wine, he explained that he wanted to give his life for and on behalf of others. He went to his death as the final act of a life of service. In raising him from the dead, God affirmed that the way Jesus lived his life – the way of service to others and self-transcendence – is the way to full human fulfilment and happiness.

This is 'good news' for us today because Jesus is *the* communion of divine and human. Now human beings know what they can and should be with the help of God's grace. He is who and what human persons are called and invited to become. At his resurrection, Jesus became God's life-giving Spirit *for us*.[27] Through Christ, and in the Spirit, God shares out God's very own life and is present to each and every one of us, in all the circumstances of our lives. God's Holy Spirit is constantly available to us, encouraging us to grow and develop, consoling us in suffering and failure, enabling us to reach the fullness of our capabilities, empowering us to become like God (*theosis*) and calling us to a life of partnership, right relationship and communion with everyone and everything in God's creation. Christian faith is about responding in freedom to God's personal invitation to love, accepting the presence of the Spirit, and living in just relationship with each other and with the created world. Men and women image God when they live as Jesus lived and so are capable of complete mutuality, equality, reciprocity and love.

The Catholic school invites children to find the inspiration for their lives in the words and the example of Jesus, to develop a relationship with him in liturgy and prayer, to live out of the gospel call to love God and neighbour, and to see themselves as being called to participate in the building of the Kingdom of God. This means that children are formed in the values and commitments of people who are followers of Jesus such as love of self and others, endless compassion, presence, forgiveness, self-sacrifice, openness to the will of God, justice, and a willingness to offer prophetic witness to the Kingdom of God. Children are challenged towards freedom and responsibility in all aspects of their lives and are taught to demonstrate Christian hospitality in imitation of Jesus.[28]

In Catholic schools 'the principal decisions and policies of the school should be referred to both the teaching and the person of Christ', such that Christian values, perspectives and attitudes have a real impact on the day to day running of the school.[29] For example, Catholic educators will tend to resist educational policies and approaches that are excessively individualistic and that emphasise personal autonomy over all other considerations. The leadership style adopted by the principal should mirror the radical inclusivity, mutuality and equality modelled by Jesus in his personal relationships. Principals will model the presence of Jesus by instilling confidence in students and colleagues and by enabling staff to exercise and develop their gifts. This might mean, for example, allowing a staff member to develop a project in an area of personal interest, or supporting a newly appointed staff member in learning time-management skills.[30]

Similarly, Jesus' tender, compassionate and forgiving presence and his particular love for the poor should have a direct impact on the way the Catholic school approaches teacher appraisal, pupil assessment, pupil discipline, enrolment policies, resource allocation, support for those with special needs, pastoral care, religious diversity, as well as the evaluation and celebration of pupils' work.[31] In all of these areas the virtues of charity, compassion, hope, justice and faith in the basic dignity and goodness of people will always triumph over attempts to define people, their work and behaviour with empirical measures of competence and bureaucratic means of control.

In the context of a Church community which serves the world

In the Catholic faith we meet God through the mediation of a community of faith, and not in isolation from one another.[32] The Catholic school could be seen as one public expression of a people's faith in a God whose presence permeates everything they do. Jesus clearly wanted to form a 'people of God' who would become signs of God in their care for all persons and all creation. The Church, as a community of the disciples of Jesus, is called to participate in God's saving work in the world today. The essence of the Church's mission, founded on God's love, is not a desire for self-preservation as a society by the imposition of its creeds and teachings. As the Congregation for Catholic Education explains: 'the Church is not an end in itself, it exists to show God to the world; it exists for others'.[33] Through word, sacrament and practical action, the Church affirms that God is salvifically present in the world, bringing about justice, peace and healing for all. Catholic schools participate in this evangelising mission of the Church, drawing people's attention to the healing presence of God, with special attention to those who are weakest.[34]

As Catholics believe in God's unconditional love for all, they will confirm that belief by a mission of preferential love for anyone who is poor and oppressed, excluded, or voiceless.[35] Because of this particular commitment, one would not only expect to find more Catholic schools in areas of poverty and educational disadvantage, but that within *all* Catholic schools, children who are on the margins will be given particular attention and care. Furthermore, it is to be expected that Catholic schools will be just communities that prepare students to work for social justice and peace on earth, until the time when God will rule over all things.[36] And the reason for all their actions for charity, justice and peace will be found in the students' relationship in faith and hope with a God of love, whom they encounter in a special way in communal celebration.

Because of the communal nature of Christianity, there should be a strong emphasis on maintaining a community atmosphere in Catholic schools, one that is enlivened by the gospel values of love, compassion, forgiveness, thirst for justice, mutuality and equality. Teachers will be invited to see their job not only as a profession but also as a *vocation*: part of the missionary work of the Church.[37] As part of a Church community which is called to be a living witness of the love of God among us, Catholic teachers will witness to the universal, inclusive and welcoming nature of Catholicism and to the value Catholicism places on ecumenism and interfaith dialogue.[38] A feature of every Catholic school should be a genuine attempt to enter into dialogue with the diverse cultures and spiritualities of *all* the students in the school.[39]

Likewise, children in Catholic schools will be invited to understand their freedom and responsibility to play their own unique part in God's work in the world. Catholics believe that we humans, through our choices and work, actively cooperate with God's work of salvation in the world and that all of these actions will be caught up in God's renewal of all creation at the end of time. Catholic education will prepare people to take an active role in social life as good citizens who respect the state, its laws and its representatives, and who promote the common good.[40] The Congregation for Catholic Education advises that children also be taught 'to discern, in the light of the Gospel, what is positive in the world, what needs to be transformed and what injustices must be overcome', adding that, 'within the context of globalization, people must be formed in such a way as to respect the identity, culture, history, religion and especially the suffering and needs of others, conscious that we are all really responsible for all'.[41]

The following checklist is offered as a summary of the distinguishing features of Catholic education as outlined in this chapter.

Checklist: Is it a Catholic school?

» **Does it offer a holistic and integral education?** Is every child treated with dignity and is education carried out within a transcendent horizon? Is every child enabled to develop to his or her full potential, including the spiritual, moral and religious dimensions of human development?

» **Does it celebrate God's reign?** Do a significant number of people in the school believe in the presence of God? Are children encouraged to become 'beholders' of grace and love in the world, noticing traces of the Divine, reaching out to others on a local and global level?

» **Does it place Jesus Christ at the centre?** Are children educated in the gospel of Jesus Christ, and offered a chance to celebrate his presence in the liturgy? Is Jesus offered as a credible model for pupils' spiritual and moral development? Does the teaching and the person of Christ have any real impact on the principal decisions and policies of the school?

» **Is it a community serving the mission of the Church in the world?** Are the gospel values in evidence in a real way? Does the school participate in the mission of the Church in the local community? Does the school reach out to all people interested in building a world founded on justice, truth and love? Are students prepared to serve the common good and to work for social justice in society? Is the school open to the admission of pupils of all religious traditions and stances for living?

Questions for reflection

» What was your understanding of Catholic education before you read this chapter? How many of your assumptions are confirmed and/or challenged by what you read? Which aspects of this theological vision resonate with you? Which aspects would you find challenging?

» Why might the Catholic community wish to establish and maintain separate schooling, rather than to provide additional religious education after mainstream schooling?

» What policies and practices would you propose by which the aims of a Catholic school could be pursued? What difference would it make to discipline policies and practice, to approaches to teacher and pupil appraisal and to approaches to inclusion of children of other religious traditions and stances for living?

» How might the example of Jesus influence leadership styles, discipline and assessment policies, and the allocation of resources in a Catholic school?

» How do the Catholic schools you know differ from the ideal image of Catholic schools as portrayed in Church documentation and in this essay?

Supplementary reading

» Vatican II, 'Declaration on Christian Education' (*Gravissimum Educationis*) 1965, in Walter Abbott, (ed.), *The Documents of Vatican II* (London: Geoffrey Chapman, 1967).

» Documents of the Congregation for Catholic Education (all available on the Vatican website: www.vatican.va) and in Leonard Franchi, (ed.), *An Anthology of Catholic Teaching on Education* (London: Scepter, 2007).

» *The Catholic School* (1977); *Lay Catholics in Schools: Witnesses of Faith* (1982); *Educational Guidance in Human Love; Outlines for Sex Education* (1983); *The Religious Dimension of Education in a Catholic School* (1988); *The Catholic School on the Threshold of the Third Millennium* (1997); *Consecrated Persons and their Mission in Schools, Reflections and Guidelines* (2002); *Educating Together in Catholic Schools* (2007); *Educating to Intercultural Dialogue in Catholic Schools: Living in Harmony for a Civilization of Love* (2013).

» John Paul II, *Catechesis Tradendae* (1979).

» Congregation for the Clergy, *General Directory for Catechesis* (1997).

» For a good summary of documentation on *Catholic Education* see John Sullivan, *Catholic Education: Distinctive and Inclusive* (Dordrecht: Kluwer, 2001), Chapter 4.

» John Sullivan and Stephen J. McKinney, *Education in a Catholic Perspective* (Farnham, Surrey: Ashgate, 2013)

» Jim Gallagher, *Serving The Young: Our Catholic Schools Today* (Bolton: Dun Bosco Publications, 2002).

Websites on Catholic education

» Catholic Education an Irish Schools Trust (CEIST): www.ceist.ie
» 'Catholic education and formation' on Irish Catholic Bishop's Conference website: www.Catholicbishops.ie
» The Catholic Education Resource Centre: www.catholiceducation.org

Endnotes

1. Fayette Breaux Veverka, 'Practicing Faith: Negotiating Identity and Difference in a Religiously Pluralistic World', *Religious Education* (2004), 99(1): 47.
2. Louis Dupré, 'Catholic Education and the Predicament of Modern Culture' in *The Living Light* (1988) March, 303.
3. Michael J. Himes, 'Living Conversation: Higher Education in a Catholic Context', *Conversations on Jesuit Higher Education* (1995), 8: 22.
4. Himes, ibid., 24.
5. For a detailed and nuanced explanation of this point see Sullivan, ibid., 78–80.
6. 'It would be wrong to consider (individual subjects) as mere adjuncts to faith or as a useful means of teaching apologetics', Congregation for Catholic Education, 'The Catholic School', 1977, no 39. For discussion of this point, see Sullivan, ibid., 86–8.
7. When we say children are 'essentially or intrinsically religious' we are not speaking of the actual religious affiliation of children: we are concerned with a deeper level of reality than that which can be empirically measured and observed. We're making what we term an ontological or metaphysical claim. Christian Smith, 'Man the Religious Animal: we are naturally but not necessarily religious', found at http://www.firstthings.com/2012/04man-the-religious-animal (accessed on 20 October 2014).
8. Pope Benedict XVI, 'Address of his Holiness Benedict XVI to the Catholic Religion Teachers', Saturday, 25 April, 2009, 2. Available on the Vatican website: www.vatican.va.
9. Congregation for Catholic Education, 'Consecrated Persons', no. 53.
10. Curtis L. Hancock, *Recovering a Catholic Philosophy of Elementary Education* (Mount Pocono, PA: Newman House Press, 2005), 38–9.
11. Congregation for Catholic Education, 'Consecrated Persons and Their Mission in Schools', 2002, no. 35.
12. Congregation for Catholic Education, 'Educating Today and Tomorrow: a Renewing Passion', *Instrumentum Laboris*, 2014', 12.
13. Congregation for Catholic Education, 'Education Together in Catholic Schools', 2007, no. 40.
14. For this point I am indebted to Sullivan's discussion of John Redden and Francis Ryan, *A Catholic Philosophy of Education* (Milwaukee, The Bruce Publishing Company, 1956), vii, 22, 29. Sullivan, ibid., 112, 117.
15. For a reflection on the Catholic emphasis on the essential goodness of human persons and the Catholic interpretation of Original Sin, see Thomas H. Groome, *Educating for Life* (Allen, Texas: Thomas More, 1998), 76–7.
16. Michael Himes, 'Living Conversation', 25.

17. Brian J. Kelty, 'Toward a Theology of Catholic Education', *Religious Education* (1999), 94(1): 15; Congregation for Catholic Education, 'Lay Catholics in Schools: Witnesses to Faith', 1982, 8, 9, 11, 12, 13, 14, 17.

18. John Sullivan, *Catholic Education: Distinctive and Inclusive* (Dordrecht: Kluwer Academic Publishers, 2001), 82.

19. Vatican II, 'Pastoral Constitution on the Church in the Modern World' (*Gaudium et Spes*), 1965, no. 35. See also Donal Murray, *A Special Concern: The Philosophy of Education: A Christian Perspective* (Dublin: Veritas, 1991), 6. See also Congregation for Catholic Education, 'The Catholic School', no 56.

20. Murray, ibid., 19

21. Sullivan, ibid., 85.

22. Sullivan, ibid., 64.

23. Joseph Cardinal Ratzinger, 'The New Evangelization: Building the Civilization of Love', Address to Catechists and Religion Teachers', 12 December, 2000, 6. Available on the Vatican website www.vatican.va.

24. Monica K. Hellwig, *Jesus the Compassion of God* (Collegeville, Minnesota: The Liturgical Press, 1983), 76ff.

25. Jon Sobrino, *Jesus the Liberator*, 2nd edn. (Maryknoll, New York: Orbis Books, 1998), 99.

26. Roger Haight, *Jesus; Symbol of God* (Maryknoll, New York: Orbis Books, 1998), 85.

27. Catherine Mowry LaCugna, *God for us: The Trinity and Christian Life* (New York: HarperSanFrancisco, 1991), 297.

28. Parramatta Diocesan Schools Board, *Freedom and Responsibility: an ethical perspective on the mission of Catholic Education* (Parramatta: PDSB, 1996), 10.

29. Sullivan, ibid., 77.

30. Parramatta Diocesan Schools Board, ibid., 11

31. Sullivan, ibid., 119.

32. Sullivan, ibid., 66.

33. Congregation for Catholic Education, 'Education Together in Catholic Schools', no. 45.

34. Vatican II, 'Declaration on Christian Education' (*Gravissimum Educationis*), no. 3.

35. Congregation for Catholic Education, 'The Catholic School on the Threshold of the Third Millennium', 1997, nos. 15 and 16.

36. Kelty, ibid., 17.

37. Congregation for Catholic Education, 'Lay Catholics', nos. 22, 24, 33, 34, 35, 41. Congregation for Catholic Education, 'The Religious Dimension', no. 96.

38. Congregation for Catholic Education, 'The Religious Dimension', no. 6; Irish Catholic Bishops' Conference, *Catholic Primary Schools: a policy for Provision into the future* (Dublin:Veritas, 2007), 5. On the Church's teaching on how Catholics relate to people of other faiths and none, see Vatican II, 'Nostra Aetate', 1968, sections 2 and 4, and Congregation for Catholic Education, 'Educating to Intercultural Dialogue in Catholic Schools: Living in Harmony for a Civilization of Love', 2013.

39. Anne Hession, 'Inter-religious Education and the Future of Religious Education in Catholic Primary Schools' in Gareth Byrne and Patricia Kieran (eds), *Toward Mutual Ground: Pluralism, Religious Education and Diversity in Irish Schools* (Dublin: Columba Press, 2013), 165-173.

40. Congregation for Catholic Education,' The Religious Dimension', no. 45; Congregation for Catholic Education, 'Education together in Catholic Schools', no. 42.

41. Congregation for Catholic Education, 'Education Together in Catholic Schools', nos. 44 and 46.

SECTION TWO
TOWARD A PUBLIC LANGUAGE OF RELIGIOUS EDUCATION FOR PRIMARY LEVEL

CHAPTER THREE
UNDERSTANDING RELIGIOUS EDUCATION

Religious Education matters because it offers an opportunity for pupils to challenge prevailing anti-religious assumptions which are common in the West. As such it is a powerful anti-indoctrinatory subject promoting thinking in depth.[1]

BRENDA WATSON

The greatest threat to children in modern liberal societies is not that they will believe in something too deeply, but that they will believe in nothing very deeply at all.[2]

WILLIAM GALSTON

The questions which our pupils ask of religion are important, but even more significant are the questions which spirituality asks of them. What matters is not only that they question, but that they are questioned. In the whole curriculum young people are encouraged to search for meaning. It is only in religious education that the possibility arises of there being meaning in search of them.[3]

JOHN M. HULL

THE WAY RELIGIOUS EDUCATION IS UNDERSTOOD IN ANY SCHOOL reflects a particular view of the religious, spiritual and ethical dimensions of human experience and a particular view of education. This chapter describes the academic discipline of religious education drawing on the public language of religious education used by those engaged in the discipline worldwide. The chapter begins with a brief examination of the concept of *religion*, and raises the question of what happens when *religion* is brought into dialogue with *education*. An understanding of religion is proposed as the basis for developing a common public language for primary religious education in the Irish context, whether it is practised in denominational, non-denominational or multi-denominational schools. It is argued that the key to the development of such a language is consideration of what the curriculum subject '*religious education*' might contribute to the personal development or humanisation[4] of the student, thus making an important contribution to their overall education in school. It is proposed that religious education introduces children to unique resources for the formation and transformation of individuals and of their communities.

When 'religion' meets 'education'

It is important to establish clearly what religious educators and curriculum policy-makers mean by the term 'religion', especially since particular approaches to the study of religion (anthropological, sociological, historical, theological, philosophical, psychological) lend themselves to particular kinds of educational programmes.[5] In education, religion(s) may be represented, for example, as metaphysical worldviews, as cultural systems,[6] as sources of social bonding and identity, as traditions of spiritual wisdom for life, as belief systems,[7] as 'world religions', as 'ways of life', as 'ways of salvation' or as 'beliefs in and/or expressions of the Sacred'.[8] There are significant differences between each of these understandings of religion with important implications for both the *content* and *process* of religious education. Further, the approach to religion taken will vary depending on whether religious education is being taught in the context of a non-denominational, inter-denominational, multi-denominational or a denominational school and whether religious denominations play a shaping role in the religious education curriculum offered. Thus, in denominational schools, the focus is on religious education in one particular denomination or religious tradition, with varying levels of attention paid to alternative religious views. In non-denominational schools, on the other hand, religious education may happen in a context in which people explore religious questions and issues, drawing from the resources of three or four different religious and perhaps even non-religious worldviews.[9]

One clear distinction is between those approaches to religious education which view religion predominantly as an object to be looked at from the perspective of secular reason and those approaches which emphasise religion as a way of life.[10] In the former case, the rational understanding and search for meaning of the learner is emphasised. In the latter, the possibility of meeting the divine (or transcendent other) in an interpersonal encounter, structured and conditioned by the conceptual beliefs, rituals, symbols, ceremonies and texts of a religious tradition, together with the engagement of the students' reason in relation to this religion, is the primary focus of the educational process.[11] Thus, for Christians, for example, being educated in religion is opening oneself to the possibility of entering into relation with God, in an intimate 'I-Thou moment' such that one's relationship with God affects one's knowing, feelings and actions in the world.

The table below distinguishes approaches which instrumentalise religion in religious education from approaches which emphasise the encounter with religion as a path to salvation.

Table 3: Approaching Religion in Religious Education.[12]

Religion as Object to be understood.	Religion as Subject to be encountered.
Third person perspective and individual experience of religion is emphasised.	First person perspective and communal experience of religion emphasised.
Emphasis on reason.	Emphasis on reason informed by revelation.
Doing religious education with an instrumental purpose: engaging with religion(s) is a means to an end, e.g. self-knowledge, spiritual and moral development, personal meaning, cultural knowledge, tolerance, inclusion and social harmony, healthy pluralism, multiculturalism, social cohesion, citizenship, democracy, etc.	Doing religious education for religion's intrinsic value, i.e. it offers salvation. Engaging with the Holy/Sacred is the goal. Responding to the gift of a divine revelation is the end. Knowing tends to lead to ethical action, (e.g. social justice, inter-religious dialogue) in the world.

Another important distinction is between those schools which represent religion(s) as particular and exclusive and those which present religious traditions as 'equal and complementary ways of experiencing the sacred' or as equal paths to salvation.[13] In secular schools, for example, the doctrinal differences between religious traditions may be downplayed in the interests of respect for difference, tolerance and social cohesion.[14] Here religions may be looked at through the lens of international human rights law or the perspective of religious freedom, for example.[15] In faith-based or denominational schools, on the other hand, as John Sullivan notes, there is more of an opportunity for students to remain 'under the umbrella' of a particular living religious tradition, 'to spend an extended period of time thinking according to its conceptual categories, evaluating experiences from its vantage point, looking out at the world from a particular angle, familiarising themselves with a particular story, internalising a set of practices, etc.'[16] Here the conceptual interpretation of religious experience in particular doctrines and beliefs has priority and the particular religion in question is understood to be more true than any other religious path. In either context, and in order to avoid the misrepresentation of religion in education, it would seem important that educators take a stand on what they think *religion* contributes to a child's overall *education*.

What does 'religion' bring to 'education'?

In Chapter One I explored the idea that education is essentially about personal development within the context of defined communities and particular traditions of values. All schools, I argued, form children in a certain vison of what it means to be human, and to live a good life. The question arises therefore as to what religion might contribute to the personal development or humanisation of students, thereby making an important contribution to their overall education in school. One way of approaching this question is to consider what it is that religions bring to the curriculum that might distinguish religious education from other subjects. Geoff Teece argues that religion is distinctive because of its *spiritual* dimension, understood as 'human transformation in the context of response to the transcendent'.[17] Here, Teece is using the term 'transcendent' to refer to something which is distinct from the universe, which cannot altogether be grasped or understood by human cognition or thought and which people nevertheless experience as a power or source of life that profoundly shapes the way they live.[18] Rowan Williams gets to the heart of this experience when he describes it as 'an experience that something (or someone) is given or bestowed which both enables and requires an answer'.[19] In other words, a religious person is one who acknowledges that 'there is more to anything and anyone I encounter than I can manage or understand' and that 'an agency independent of any circumstance within the world has "taken responsibility" for *my* welfare – has not only given life in general, but put at my disposal the life that is its own'.[20] To be religious, then, is to acknowledge a dependence, and even indebtedness, to something beyond yourself and to live your life in the knowledge that the deepest meaning and truth is found in allowing oneself to become part of that larger supernatural reality (e.g. God/Allah/Brahman/Dharma) which has been encountered. It is an understanding of this belief in a transcendent or supernatural reality structured by the unique language and practices of particular religions that uniquely distinguishes the discipline of religious education from other subjects on the curriculum, providing distinctive contributions to the spiritual, moral and religious dimensions of personal development with which education is concerned.[21]

Honouring the nature of 'religion' in religious education

The religious person adopts a certain vision of transcendent reality, of the world and of the human person as that which is truly true or really real. This vision, as Terrence Merrigan notes, is for many people comprehensive and incapable of abandonment.[22] For many religious people, their belief in the transcendent and their understanding of what is true about themselves and about reality is fundamental to their lives. Their acknowledgement of transcendent experience and the particular beliefs and practices which structure that experience does not merely influence their inner or private life. Religion shapes *all* of their decisions, providing an ideal of conduct and character to which they aspire. It will impact upon how they live, how they spend their money, the kind of work they do, the way they approach their work, the values they cherish, the ways they participate in the community, how they approach suffering and death, how they vote, and what they do in their spare time.

A religious vision is ultimate and is not easily abandoned without a serious psychological crisis or some sort of conversion experience. As Jeff Astley explains:

> The point of religion lies primarily in its spiritual power. Thus religious concepts should not be interpreted as neutral portrayals of transcendent realities and processes, which we coolly adopt or drop depending on the extent to which they cohere with our framework of 'truth claims'. They are effective concepts that lead to a sense of spiritual wholeness and salvation. They are contained in beliefs that have been framed to drive spiritual and moral lives – doctrines to live

and to die for. Most religious concepts are saturated with religious affect. Within Christianity, for example, the doctrine of creation is inextricably linked with feelings of dependence and gratitude; the concept of God's presence with awe and the flavour of grace; and claims about the resurrection with a sense of meaning and hope. Hence, the clarification of these religious concepts within the Church's religious teaching is not some sort of austere intellectual exercise, but a process that is intended both to define and to generate spiritual attitudes, insight and response.[23]

When religion is understood in this fashion, the practice of religious education cannot be seen as a matter of laying out the options for children and letting them choose whichever set of beliefs, stories or practices they feel drawn to. As L. Philip Barnes has pointed out, this is to fundamentally misrepresent religion in education, because it accords too strong a role to critical reason in the actual process by which a people learn *in* and *from* religion for their lives. In sum, the task is to find a representation of religion in religious education that is closer to what religion actually is. All religious education should help children understand and appreciate religious experiences, doctrines, beliefs and practices and their place in the lives of individuals and societies.[24]

Religious education for transformation
For many religious persons, the point of religion is about ongoing transformation or 'conversion': learning how to see and experience the self, others and the world

94

differently because of what has been encountered and what they believe to be true about the nature of reality. Thus, for example, to be a Christian calls for a re-envisioning of oneself as a disciple of Jesus and seeing oneself as living in unity with God. Hence the highest goal in becoming human, for a Christian, may involve losing many of the false trappings of the ego in order to gain the freedom of living according to God's purposes in the world. In other words being religious for a Christian leads to a re-reading or a new reading of oneself, of the world and of one's values, starting with reference to God.

This idea of conversion or personal transcendence is found at the heart of many of the world's religions. In Buddhism, for example, the change is a realisation of the illusory nature of the 'self'; in Judaism we find the concept of teshuvah, 'turning around'; in Christianity there is the concept of 'putting on Christ Jesus'; in Islam we find the concept of a reversion to one's natural inclination (fitah) as a Muslim. Typically the goal of personal transcendence entails engaging in specific practices (fasting, self-sacrifice, reflection, ritual, prayer) which bring religious people closer to what they consider to be real and true. They immerse themselves in certain images and stories such that they affect their feelings, their attitudes and their behaviours; they trust in certain beliefs which provide them with a more or less comprehensive understanding of the meaning of life; they place their hope in a specific view of the present world and of its future; and they understand their own identity and their life with others as having an additional meaning because of their experience of transcendence and their response to it.

Religious education

Religious education can be understood as an academic discipline which invites the student to personal transcendence leading to personal and social transformation. Religious education invites students to examine and learn the dynamic of personal transcendence; enabling them to develop ways of thinking, feeling and doing which alter their experiences of themselves, others and the world. The emphasis in religious education should be on teaching people to draw on spiritual traditions of wisdom for their own lives and the lives of others. Whatever the context of religious education, schools should invite children to connect what they know with the person they are becoming.[25] Students should be invited to push beyond simply learning about religious traditions (their key figures, doctrines, texts, rituals, practices, etc.) to experience, understand, judge and decide how religious understandings, doctrines, moral principles and practices affect their own lives. In this way all religious education will be informative and deeply formative at the same time.[26]

Good religious education will invite the pupil, not only to develop their knowledge and understanding of religion(s), but to a new way of being and acting, a new sense of self and other. As Gabriel Moran has argued, the religiously educated person will learn how to transcend themselves, how to detach their spirit from their ego, how to identify themselves with all of humanity and in communion with the earth. Thus, says Moran, when people are religiously educated in a healthy way it should lead to genuine reverence for others and for the earth.[27]

In sum, religious education can be defined as follows: any educational process by which people are invited to explore the human religious traditions that protect and illuminate the experience of belief in transcendence/the divine, leading to personal and social transformation.

When viewed in this manner religious education is *not* about getting children to accept propositions or doctrines which will determine their behaviour, *not* about learning lots of facts about religions, *not* about having 'a religion' or having a sense of themselves as Catholic or Muslim, or Buddhist, over and against everyone else.[28] Instead, those who learn either *in* or *from* a religion in religious education might be expected to become aware of, understand and respond to the fact that life can be lived with an awareness of something which calls us beyond what we can fully grasp, control or know, and that to live in relation to this transcendent dimension brings about personal and social transformation.

Note also that this understanding of religious education requires that good religious education will contribute, not only to the personal lives of citizens, but also to the vitality of the public space. Those who are religiously educated should be strengthened in their capacity to act for the transformation of their communities. This is because religions are an important source of healthy cultural identity and political formation for citizens in society.[29] As Richard Pring argues, '[t]he common good is served better by those who are deeply rooted in the very best of the different traditions of the communities that make up society'. This is because religious traditions are 'crucial to the maintenance of a moral and social perspective through which so many young people might be enabled to gain a sense of identity, a story which gives them a feeling of dignity and self-worth, a richness from which they can contribute to the common good'.[30] Indeed, it could also be argued that people are more likely to be genuinely tolerant and respectful of difference when they are securely rooted in their own distinctive beliefs, values and identity.[31] Most of the principal religious traditions in the world require of their adherents belief in some variant of the golden rule and many religious traditions have within their ethical framework an imperative to treat people of other religions with respect. For example, the imperative to love the neighbour and the stranger is found at the heart of Jewish and Christian faith. School-based religious education has an important role to play in ensuring that children are introduced to the resources of religious moralities both for their personal development and for the social development of communities.[32]

Religious education and indoctrination

Religious education, wherever it is practised, must be rooted in educational practices which respect the freedom of the learner. As a discipline, it is firmly opposed to indoctrination. Indoctrination can be understood as teaching someone to accept ideas, beliefs, doctrines and practices uncritically, to the exclusion of other points of view. Thus one could experience religious indoctrination or secular indoctrination, for example. When used in the context of religious education, indoctrination often conveys the connotation of brainwashing: pressurising or persuading a person into beliefs, forbidding criticism and giving a partial or distorted view of things.[33] Donal Murray proposes, alternatively, that we view indoctrination as 'presenting a world-view while protesting, no doubt sincerely that one is not doing so'.[34] One of the perennial features in the use of the term 'indoctrination' is that it is invariably used to describe what the 'other' is doing and hence the need for wariness in relation to the political uses to which the term is subjected.[35]

According to the German philosopher of education, Jürgen Oelkers, 'we have only one criterion for whether education is indoctrination or not, the criterion of understanding'.[36] Elmer J. Thiessen agrees, noting that 'the curtailment of a person's growth towards normal rational autonomy' is the 'core idea of indoctrination'.[37] 'Successful indoctrination', adds Gabriel Moran, 'results in a person so attached to one version of reality that multiple perspectives, ambiguity in language and the ability to stand at a difference from one's own beliefs, have been eliminated'.[38] To ensure that this does not occur, there must always be a place for questioning, critical thought and the giving of reasons in *all* forms of religious education in Irish primary schools. Religious educators have an important role to play in ensuring that children learn how to use their reason in the domain of religion. When religion is excluded from education or when people are taught to be religious in an uncritical way the problems of bigotry, sectarianism, parochialism, fundamentalism and anti-religious attitudes are allowed to fester.

It is important to distinguish indoctrination from legitimate educational practices of formation and nurture.[39] There will always be an element of transmission, enculturation and formation involved in passing on distinctive ways of life and worldviews to young children. This is true whether the value commitments, practices, symbols and beliefs in question are religious or secular. In this sense, all schools induct children into various traditions of life and thought and it is incorrect to describe such socialisation processes as indoctrination. It will of course be important that, as children develop, all schools will allow them to critically reflect on and creatively transform the traditions into which they have been initiated.[40] This is because education by its nature entails freedom of thought, inquiry, questioning, reason, judgement and critical openness. Therefore, those who seek to initiate children either into a secular worldview or a religious worldview will always be wary of educational practices that do not allow for flexible thinking and legitimate questioning. All approaches to religious or ethical education should invite the active participation of students in thinking critically and creatively, reaching conclusions and forming attitudes and values. People who have been taught in such a way that they ultimately are not capable of evaluating their own worldview – religious or secular – are people who have not been educated at all.

Denominational, multi-denominational and non-denominational primary religious education programmes should be distinguished from indoctrination when the religious freedom of children is respected, when children are invited to bring reason into dialogue with religious and secular traditions, when the spiritual, moral and religious needs and capacities of children inform the curriculum, when they include some age-appropriate teaching about religions/worldviews other than the children's own and when children are taught about the religious/secular worldview in which they are being nurtured in a manner suited to their psychological stage of development.

Religious education from an international perspective

Religious education in the public space is now carried out in accordance with European and international human rights legislation. All religious education should respect the rights of freedom of religion or belief within the law as advocated in Article 18 of the Universal Declaration of Human Rights (1948), the United Nations Declaration on the Elimination of All Forms of Intolerance and of Discrimination Based on Religion or Belief (1981) and Article 18 of the International Covenant on Civil and Political Rights (ratified by Ireland in 1989). Article 18 states that '[e]veryone shall have the right to freedom of thought, conscience and religion'. However, as Andrew McGrady notes, 'freedom of religion relates to both freedom "for" religion and freedom "from" religion' and 'both must be acknowledged and accommodated within any and every approach to teaching religion'.[41]

Education for responsible religious and ethical pluralism is now an integral part of religious education at every level. Furthermore, it is now seen as preferable that young people develop their religious identity in the context of a developing concept of active citizenship at national, European and even world levels.[42] This means that all children be invited to reconcile their citizenship of Ireland, Europe and the world with their religious beliefs or other stances for living. Some guidelines that inform religious education in a European context are The 'Toledo Guiding Principles on Teaching about Religions and Beliefs in Public Schools' (2007) and 'Signposts- Policy and Practice for Teaching about Religions and Non-religious worldviews in Intercultural Education' (2014).[43]

Commenting on the importance of the international and European human rights framework within which all religious education in the public space is now considered, Andrew McGrady affirms that:

> The minimum acceptable outcomes for the religiously educated person, irrespective of the context or the extent of that education, is a person who relates his or her personal religion or conviction to the authentic values of democratic society, who is religious or convinced in a manner that is tolerant towards and deeply appreciative of the 'other', exercises her or his right to religious freedom in a moderate way that is in solidarity with the right of others, particularly members of minority religions, to religious freedom, and who is committed to active citizenship, locally, nationally and globally. To achieve this religious education must uphold and promote human rights, reflect critically upon the contribution of religion to democratic society, see the various religious heritages of humankind as a shared heritage, assist the learner to critique his or her personal religious culture (or culture of conviction), and actively engage in intercultural and interreligious dialogue.[44]

Summary: is it religious education?

Religious education:

» attends to the formation and transformation of the individual and of the community.

» contributes to the moral, social and spiritual development of pupils.

» draws children's attention to the *spiritual* dimension of life, understood as relationship to the transcendent or the divine.

» enables understanding and appreciation of religious experience, religious language, religious beliefs and religious practices and their place in life, both personal and social.

» reflects faithfully the way in which students experience and understand their religious commitments.

» enables students to draw on spiritual traditions of wisdom for their own lives and the lives of others.

» enables students to discern how being religious in a healthy way entails serving the common good, human dignity, justice and peace.

» is rooted in educational practices which respect the freedom of conscience and freedom of religion of the learner.

» is carried out in accordance with European and international human rights legislation.

» prepares students for responsible religious and ethical pluralism.

Conclusion

In Ireland, we are witnessing the development of a new discourse on *primary* religious education in the public sphere.[45] This chapter proposes that religious education be viewed as an academic discipline that attends to the formation and transformation of individuals and communities. Tensions inevitably arise when religion is brought into the domain of education and when educational considerations seem to conflict with the self-understanding of religious people and traditions. Nevertheless, attention to the numerous contexts within which contemporary religious education is now carried out (Church and State, Irish society, European and International contexts) should enable all those concerned with religious education in Irish primary schools to come together in dialogue about the future of school-based primary religious education in the twenty-first century.

Questions for reflection

» What is religion?

» What is education?

» How should religion and education be combined? What principles should guide the bringing of religion (s) into education? Can religion be misrepresented in education?

» When religions enter education should they be considered primarily as matters of private belief and practice *or* as forms of life shared by communities?

» How do you think children can benefit from their study of religion in school? What does religious education contribute (to the personal development of the child) that is unique and that isn't contributed by other subjects such as SPHE or ethics?

» Would it be good to remove religious education from the school altogether? Why?

Supplementary reading

» The legal and human rights issues surrounding the right to withdraw from religious instruction in Ireland are discussed in Alison Mawhinney, *Freedom of Religion and Schools: the Case of Ireland* (Saarbrucken: VDM Verlag, 2009).

» A set of political principles for education about religions and beliefs in public schools in Europe is found in: Organisation for Security and Co-operation in Europe, *The Toledo guiding principles on teaching about religions and beliefs in public schools* (Warsaw: Organisation for Security and Co-operation in Europe, Office For Democratic Institutions and Human Rights). Found at http://www.osce.org/item/28314.html.

» The Council of Europe offers advice in Professor Robert Jackson, *Signposts- Policy and Practice for teaching about religions and non-religious world views in intercultural education* (Renouf Pub. Co. Ltd, 2014).

» Martin Rothgangel, Robert Jackson, and Martin Jäggle (eds), *Religious Education at Schools In Europe: Part 2: Western Europe* (Vienna: Vienna University Press at V&R unipress, 2014).

On the topic of indoctrination the following texts are helpful:

» Karl Ernst Nipkow, 'Christian Education and the Charge of Indoctrination : a German perspective' in Dennis Bates, Gloria Durka and Friedrich Schweitzer (eds), *Education, Religion and Society* (London: New York: Routledge, 2006), 103–14.

» Elmar Thiessen, *Teaching for Commitment: Liberal Education, Indoctrination and Christian Nurture* (Leominster: Gracewing, 1993).

» Liam Gearon, *MasterClass in Religious Education: Transforming Teaching and Learning* (London: Bloomsbury, 2013).

Endnotes

1. Brenda Watson, 'Why Religious Education Matters' in L. Philip Barnes (ed.), *Debates in Religious Education*, (London: Routledge, 2012), 20.

2. William Galston, 'Civic Education in the Liberal State' in Nancy L. Rosenblum, *Liberalism and the Moral Life* (Cambridge: Harvard University Press, 1989), 101.

3. John M. Hull, 'Religious Education and Personal, Social and Moral Education', printed in John M. Hull, *Utopian Whispers: moral, religious and spiritual values in schools* (London: Religious and Moral Education Press, 1998).

4. The claim here is that while we are all born human we can develop in ways that enhance our humanity (e.g. through love) or in ways that lead to dehumanisation (e.g. killing, self-destructive practices).

5.   On the study of religion as a multi-disciplinary area of enquiry, see Clive Erricker, *Religious Education: a conceptual and interdisciplinary approach for secondary level* (London: Routledge, 2010), Chapter 3.

6.   See for example the definition of ERB (Education about religion and beliefs) in John Coolahan, Caroline Hussey and Fionnuala Kilfeather (eds), *The Report of the forum on Patronage and Pluralism in the Primary Sector* (Dublin: Department of Education and Skills, 2012), v, where ERB is described as: '... a programme which helps pupils to know about and to understand the rich cultural heritage of forms of religion and beliefs which have been embraced by humankind'.

7.   See Kelleher et al., *Learn Together: an ethical education curriculum for Educate Together schools* (Dublin: Educate Together, 2004), 35–42.

8.   As Clive Erricker has pointed out, very few major contemporary theorists of religious education in Britain base their pedagogy on educational principles, in the first instance, rather than on those derived from an approach to the study of religion. See Clive Erricker, ibid., 64.

9.   At European level, for example, there has been an attempt to broaden the subject of religious education to include non-religious belief systems, in line with the human rights principle of freedom of religion or belief. The Congregation for Catholic Education's most recent guidelines, 'Educating to Intercultural Dialogue in Catholic Schools', 2013, nos., 8, 12, recommend that religions 'dialogue not only among themselves, but also with the various forms of atheistic, or non-religious interpretations of the human person and history', since these latter are also faced with the fundamental questions of meaning posed by all persons.

10. See Hanan A. Alexander, 'Autonomy, Faith and Reason: McLaughlin and Callan on religious initiation' in Graham Haydon (ed.), *Faith in Education: a tribute to Terence McLaughlin* (London: University of London, 2009), 31.

11. For the argument that religious concepts and religious language together structure and condition religious experience, see L. Philip Barnes, *Education, Religion and Diversity: Developing a new model of Religious Education* (London: Routledge, 2014), 113–16. For the argument that Christianity has its own distinctive epistemology, see Debra Dean Murphy, *Teaching that Transforms: Worship as the Heart of Christian Education* (Grand Rapids, Michigan: Brazos Press, 2004).

12. I'm indebted here to the analysis of Alexander and Ken Wilber. See Hanan A. Alexander, 'Autonomy, Faith and Reason: McLaughlin and Callan on religious initiation' in Graham Haydon (ed.), *Faith in Education: a tribute to Terence McLaughlin* (London: University of London, 2009), 27–45. See Ken Wilber's way of mapping differing approaches to the spiritual domain of experience in his *Integral Spirituality* (London: Boston, 2007).

13. See L. Philip Barnes 'Religious Education and the Misrepresentation of Religion' in Marius Felderhof, Penny Thompson, and David Torevell (eds), *Inspiring Faith in Schools* (Hampshire: Ashgate, 2007), 75–86 and his *Education, Religion and Diversity* (London: Routledge, 2014), Chapters 6–10 for a critical review of the philosophical and theological assumptions behind the phenomenological and liberal theological models of religious education.

14. L. Philip Barnes, 'Religious Education and the Misrepresentation of Religion' in Marius Felderhof et al. (eds), ibid., 75–86. A good example of this in the Irish context is the Educate Together *Learn Together* curriculum which invites children to study how 'our shared human experience' relates to 'religious beliefs systems' (see Belief Systems Strand).

15. Liam Gearon, *MasterClass in Religious Education: Transforming Teaching and Learning* (London: Bloomsbury, 2013), 18. *The Toledo Guiding Principles on Teaching about Religions and Beliefs in Public Schools* (OSCE, 2007) offers one human rights framework for teaching about religions and beliefs.

16. John Sullivan, 'Faith Schools: a culture within a culture in a changing world' in M. de Souza et al. (eds), *International Handbook of the Religious, Moral and Spiritual Dimensions in Education* (Dordrecht: Springer, 2006), 941.

17. Geoff Teece, 'Is Learning about and from religions, religion or religious education? And is it any wonder some teachers don't get it?' *British Journal of Religious Education* (2010) 32(2): 99.

18. Other terms for the transcendent include 'the Sacred', 'The Other', 'Ultimate Mystery', 'The Holy' or 'God'.

19. Rowan Williams, *Faith in the Public Square* (London: Bloomsbury, 2012), 90.

20. Williams, ibid., 5 and 90.

21. I'm indebted to L. Philip Barnes here for my understanding of religion and his identification of what is distinctive about religion, namely the claim that there is a supernatural level of reality that transcends the natural world, that belief in the divine is constitutive and distinctive of a religion and that distinctive accounts of the nature of the divine are integrated into wider forms of life that incorporate other beliefs and religious practices. L. Philip Barnes, *Education, Religion and Diversity*, 119–25.

22. Terrence Merrigan, 'Religion, Education and the Appeal to Plurality: Theological Considerations on the Contemporary European Context' in Gareth Byrne and Patricia Kieran (eds), *Toward Mutual Ground: Pluralism, Religious Education and Diversity in Irish Schools* (Dublin: The Columba Press, 2013), 57.

23. Jeff Astley, 'Crossing the Divide?' in Felderhof et al (eds), ibid., 177.

24. For the argument that representation of religions in education should reflect religions as they are for their followers, see L. Philip Barnes, ibid., 155.

25. On this vision of religious education that corresponds with the Jewish and Christian idea of biblical wisdom see Thomas H. Groome, 'Religious Ed and Catechesis – no Divorce for the Children's sake', *The Furrow* (2002), 53 (11): 594.

26. Thomas H. Groome proposes that we approach all religions as *traditions of spiritual wisdom* and teach them as resources for people's own spiritual journeys. Groome, ibid., 587–96.

27. Gabriel Moran, *Religious Education Development* (Minneapolis: Winston Press, 1983), 140f. See Padraic O'Hare, 'Gabriel Moran and Religious Education for Reverence' in *The Enduring Covenant* (Valley Forge, Pennsylvania: Trinity Press International, 1997), 101–27.

28. I'm indebted here to Gabriel Moran's distinction between 'education in a religion' and 'education for being religious'. For a summary see Padraic O'Hare, ibid., 121.

29. On the idea that modern states of themselves are unable to provide those visions of life that are strong enough to motivate ethical choices and actions for solidarity, see Jürgen Habermas, 'A Reply', in Jürgen Habermas et al, *An Awareness of What is Missing: Faith and Reason in a Post-Secular Age* (Cambridge: Polity Press, 2010), 74–5.

30. Richard Pring, 'Can Faith schools serve the Common Good?' in Graham Haydon (ed.), *Faith in Education* (London: Institute of Education, University of London, 2009), 72, 74.

31. J. Mark Halstead, 'In Defence of Faith Schools', in Graham Haydon (ed.), ibid., 56.

32. L. Philip Barnes discuss the essential role of religious education in the moral education of students in common schools (i.e. post-confessional approaches to religious education) in his *Education, Religion and Diversity*, Chapter 14.

33. Oxford English Dictionary, found at http://www.oed.com (accessed on 3 November 2014). For a helpful discussion of the charge of indoctrination levelled at confessional religious education, see L. Philip Barnes, ibid., 59–63. For a defence of the view that Christian nurture is compatible with the values and principles of liberal education see Elmer J. Thiessen, *Teaching for Commitment: Liberal Education, Indoctrination and Christian Nurture* (London: McGill-Queen's University Press, 1993).

34. Donal Murray, *The Philosophy of Education: a Christian Perspective* (Dublin: Veritas, 1991), 18.

35. I'm indebted to my colleague Dr. Jonathan Kearney for this insight.

36. J. Oelkers, 'Freedom and Learning: Some thoughts on Liberal and Progressive Education', in B. Spiecker and R. Straughtan (eds), *Freedom and Indoctrination in Education: International Perspectives* (London: Cassell, 1991), 80.

37. Thiessen, ibid., 234.

38. Gabriel Moran, *Showing How: The Act of Teaching* (Valley Forge, Pennsylvania: Trinity Press International, 1997), 86.

39. Thiessen, ibid., 205ff.

40. J. Oelkers, 'Freedom and Learning: Some Thoughts on Liberal and Progressive Education', in B. Spiecker and R. Straughan (eds), *Freedom and Indoctrination in Education: International Perspectives* (London: Cassell, 1991).

41. Andrew G. McGrady, 'Teaching Religion at Schools in Ireland' in Martin Rothgangel, Robert Jackson and Martin Jäggle (eds), *Religious Education at Schools In Europe: Part 2: Western Europe* (Vienna: Vienna University Press at V&R unipress, 2014), 130.

42. This is why some religious educators have called for Christian churches to change their national orientation into a European and global orientation. See ICCS Working Group 'Giving Europe a Heart and Soul—A Christian Vision for Education in Europe's Schools' in Peter Schreiner, Hans Spinder, Jeremy Taylor and Wim Westerman (eds), *Committed to Europe's Future: contributions from Education and Religious Education: a Reader* (Münster: Comenius Institute, 2002), 79–84.

43. OSCE, 'The Toledo guiding principles on teaching about religions and beliefs in public schools'. (Warsaw: Organisation for Security and Co-operation in Europe, Office For Democratic Institutions and Human Rights.) Found at http://www.osce.org/item/28314.html, (accessed on 3 November 2014). Professor Robert Jackson, *Signposts- Policy and Practice for teaching about Religions and Non-religious World views in Intercultural Education* (Renouf Pub. Co. Ltd, 2014).

44. Andrew McGrady, 'Religious Education, Citizenship and Human Rights: Perspectives from the United Nations and the Council of Europe' in M. de Souza et al. (eds), ibid., 990–1.

45. Sandra Cullen provides an interesting introduction to the four publics to which religious education has to be accountable: the State, the Church, the academy and the person. Sandra Cullen, 'Toward an Appropriate Religious Education for Future Teachers of Religious Education: Principles for a Theological Education Approach', Doctoral Thesis (2013), Dublin City University, unpublished.

CHAPTER FOUR
APPROACHES TO RELIGIOUS EDUCATION

In a strict sense, no course — whether on religion or on any other subject — is absolutely neutral or objective: rather there is in fact a spectrum of possibilities.[1]

TOLEDO GUIDING PRINCIPLES ON TEACHING ABOUT RELIGIONS AND BELIEFS IN PUBLIC SCHOOLS

The most common ways of doing religious education badly are to sanitise it, fudge it, moralise it.[2]

CLIVE ERRICKER

THERE ARE MANY DIFFERENT APPROACHES TO PRIMARY RELIGIOUS education. The way religious education is taught in any school reflects a particular view of the religious, spiritual and ethical dimensions of human experience and a particular view of the purposes of education. In other words, the way religion(s), beliefs and education are brought into a relationship always reflects a value-laden understanding of how pupils will benefit from their study of religion(s) and beliefs.[3] A strictly neutral, value-free approach to religious education is impossible. Every approach is value laden and every approach seeks to form children through specific content, principles and values.

When examining approaches to primary religious education it is helpful to ask the question: what does this particular model of religious education contribute to young children's spiritual, moral and/or religious development? Should religious education be concerned with helping children to learn how to *be* spiritual, moral or religious, or should religious education simply aim to increase understanding and tolerance of different religions and beliefs? Can it do both? Can religious education in a formal school setting aid children in developing their own spirituality, ethics, faith and values? If so, how?

There is a growing interest in student-centred approaches to religious education, which are concerned to answer the question, what do *young* children need from their study of religions, religious faith, worldviews, spiritualities and beliefs? What does religious education contribute to their personal development that is not offered by other subjects on the curriculum? What is the link between the domain of spirituality, ethics, religion and the development of the whole child which primary education aims to promote? Which approach to religious education best serves young children's development of identity, autonomy and religious freedom? Which approach to religion and beliefs promotes tolerance of, respect for and dialogue with other religions and cultures?

Types of religious education

In a seminal essay written in *The Blackwell Guide to the Philosophy of Education*, Hanan Alexander and Terence H. McLaughlin draw a helpful distinction between two broad conceptions of education in religion and spirituality, which they label 'education in religion and spirituality from the outside' and 'education in religion and spirituality from the inside' respectively.[4] They argue that any liberal democratic society can legitimately make provision for both kinds of education in religions and spirituality. Both types aim to form children in particular ways of thinking and in particular values and virtues; both should promote rationality and openness to other points of view; both should be rooted in good educational practices which promote dialogue with the learner's experiences, interests and needs, and both require the free assent of the learner to participate.[5] At the same time, both types need to be accountable in the public space; to draw on contemporary philosophy and the social sciences; and to enable the learner to develop personally, spiritually and ethically as an active and responsible citizen. 'Education in religion and spirituality from the outside' and 'education in religion and spirituality from the inside' will be examined below.

The two types

'Education in religion and spirituality from the outside' is typically offered in 'common' schools of liberal democratic societies. It is sometimes called non-confessional religious education. In this type the teacher introduces students to a number of religions and life stances, without emphasising any in particular. Typically, students are taught *about* some religious and spiritual traditions with the view to promoting knowledge, understanding, autonomous judgement, tolerance and respect. Such approaches tend to be underpinned by a multicultural or pluralistic philosophy of religion and are increasingly influenced by political aims in a European and international context.[6] The basic philosophical assumption here is that religions are comparable entities that can be studied side by side. As Lieven Boeve notes, this type of religious education 'presupposes fundamental life options and religions which are already able to deal with plurality and difference.'[7]

In 'Education in religion and spirituality from the outside', religious education is understood as an activity of the public space which aims primarily to empower the student with critical skills for understanding religions. The teacher may offer an understanding of the history, practices, spiritualities, and key expressions of religions (and sometimes other life stances) and their adherents using phenomenological, sociological, historical, experiential/ existential, critical realist, or constructivist methods.[8] Religion is often presented as a cultural reality that may be studied in terms of artefacts, texts, rituals, institutions, structures, leaders and beliefs.

As Robert Jackson explains, politically, proponents of this type of religious education 'affirm the individual's democratic right to freedom of religion or belief, and actively promote tolerance of religious and ideological difference within the law'.[9] In this sense religious education is seen as a discipline that supports liberal democratic political goals. McLaughlin and Alexander add that, because religions and spiritual beliefs, values and practices are seen as 'significantly controversial' in these approaches, they are understood 'as matters for the reflective evaluation, decision and response of individuals and families'.[10] This is because 'religious and spiritual belief, commitment, and practice on the part of individuals are neither presuppositions of, nor aims of, the enterprise'.[11]

Approaches to religion and spirituality 'from the outside' differ as regards the extent to which children's actual religious or other stances for living are taken into consideration. In some cases, for example, the aim is not merely that students would learn *about* religions and other stances for living but that students might learn *from* these traditions for their own spiritual, moral and/or religious lives.[12] In these cases, the intention may be to help students understand and assess religious/spiritual practices or traditions in light of their own experience of transcendence or the Sacred or their own search for spirituality, meaning, purpose, truth and values. Here religious education contributes to *self*-knowledge and *self*-identity. As Dermot Lane explains:

> Learning from religion does carry with it the possibility of some kind of change or indeed transformation – but it does not contain any intention of conversion. Furthermore, learning from religion requires the exercise of empathy and imagination – activities required in the teaching and learning of other subjects in the curriculum. Learning from religion requires an ability to walk in the shoes of the other, and therefore to

take 'seriously the seriousness of others and testing it against what one holds seriously oneself'.[13]

In 'outside' approaches, religions and worldviews are typically presented from a secular philosophical perspective. (Proponents of these approaches should not however be presumed to promote ideological secularism, a particular point of view which seeks to exclude religion from the public sphere and from education as a matter of principle.)[14] By approaching religions from a secular perspective, teachers aim to be accurate and fair in their treatment of the practices, symbols and claims of religions.[15] They are concerned to convey impartiality when it comes to competing points of view about religion and to display appropriate sensitivity when dealing with controversial matters. As a result, they are often expected to abstain from judgements about religions and are sometimes expected to bracket out their own personal religious or other commitments.[16] The teacher is expected, however, to support a secular approach to religion and to form children in the distinctive attitudes to religion that underpin the curriculum.

Approaches to religion and spirituality from the outside are often based in liberal political values and principles such as the rational autonomy of the individual, the demands of democratic citizenship, freedom of belief and tolerance of the beliefs of others, dialogue, openness to and tolerance of others, recognition of plurality and respect for singularity and difference. Boeve argues that this set of values 'principally distinguishes itself from secular neutrality, religious indifference and relativism, and religious fundamentalism'.[17] As these values and principles are commonly accepted in liberal democratic societies, they tend to be acceptable to many parents.[18]

A common understanding of learners, in this type, is that they are autonomous individuals who explore religious and secular traditions to aid them in a search for meaning in life.[19] Approaches 'from the outside' often accentuate what religions have in common and tend not to confront the student with the question of the validity of religious belief systems. The truth status of religious statements is often not addressed because, as Jackson explains, it is assumed that 'issues concerning the truth of particular religious claims cannot be resolved publicly'.[20] Furthermore, the extent to which students can be helped to experience or to name what it means to be religious or spiritual in a particular way in this context is limited, due to the particular nature of spiritual traditions (e.g. the integral relationship between spirituality and prayer in religions) and due to the obligation placed on the 'common' school not to concern itself with controversial matters.

The term 'education in religion and spirituality from the inside' refers to the forms of religious/spiritual education offered for those within a particular religious and spiritual tradition, or for those who are being initiated into such a tradition. Here students are educated in religion as something that is central to the way one lives one's entire life. It is sometimes known as faith-based, denominational or confessional religious education. It has also been described as 'learning religion',[21] or 'learning into religion'.[22] In Ireland, Christian (Catholic, Church of Ireland, Methodist, Presbyterian), Jewish and Muslim schools engage in this type of religious education. Here religious education takes place as 'a discourse both within a religious community and from the religious community to the public space'.[23]

In this form of religious education, as John Sullivan explains, 'the religion is encountered on its own terms, rather than merely as an object to be looked at through secular spectacles'.[24] Religion may be examined from the perspective of tradition, religious faith, personal involvement, mystery and the experience of religion as a gift, along with an understanding of mystery, of revelation and of truth that is discovered rather than constructed by the student. In other words, the idea that the children are invited to encounter something/someone beyond their individual subjectivity is emphasised in these approaches.

In faith-based approaches the learner is often understood as one who shares a religious tradition with a community, and as one who is invited to practise the religion with a view to coming to understanding. Children are addressed as if they are practising religious life or they are at least invited to explore what it might be like to live as religious persons. Rather than observing religion, children are invited to immerse themselves in it. The primary aim of this type of religious education is formation in the beliefs, faith and practices of the religion in question. Children learn how to think religiously, how to engage in ritual practices, how to pray, how to live ethically drawing on the resources of a religious tradition, and how to belong in community. Here, religion is 'connected to an integral way of life and the set of practices that sustain this way of life'.[25]

'Inside' approaches vary in the extent to which learners are invited to reflect critically on their own religion and to learn about other religious/spiritual paths. In the Catholic tradition, for example, while the truth of Christian faith is assumed, this does not preclude openness to the truths contained in other traditions. Thus Alexander and McLaughlin explain that, ideally, 'education in religion and spirituality from the inside' is:

> a form of education in religion and spirituality that is recognisably educational, not indoctrinatory, in that it is both supportive of religious and spiritual traditions by aiming at religious belief, faith, and practice on the part of students and also at the same time aiming at the development of a form of rational autonomy and democratic citizenship ... . [S]tudents are encouraged to put their formation into critical perspective and to make any acceptance of it on their part authentic. ... [W]hat is being aimed at is critical, authentic faith, not mere lip service.[26]

This type of religious/spiritual education is justified as an appropriate option when parents freely seek it. As Alexander and McLaughlin explain, '[t]he mandate for these forms of education in pluralist liberal democratic societies is seen as arising from the exercise of the rights of parents and religious communities in relation to the formation of their children and young people and an acknowledgement of the demands of legitimate plurality in educational arrangements'.[27]

Speaking of denominational approaches to religious education in European countries, Peter Schreiner clarifies that, '[w]here religious education is denominationally oriented, it must be emphasised that this approach is not understood as the consequence of a state church or of a majority religion. Rather it is considered the realisation of state neutrality and the individual freedom of religion'.[28] Increasingly, this kind of religious education is also being justified by some commentators, on the grounds of the right of children to be educated in their own religion.[29]

The principles and values that underpin faith-based approaches include: beliefs about God and about the path to salvation; beliefs about human nature (such as the person's destiny after death); beliefs about the world, religious freedom, commitment to truth, faithfulness to tradition, religious autonomy and moral autonomy. Politically, these approaches may seek to preserve a particular religious patrimony and a distinctive philosophy of education. For example, Catholic schools emphasise an understanding of education as the transformation of persons in the context of a religious community which aims to serve the common good of the whole society. Ethically, proponents of these approaches are often concerned to be faithful to the religious tradition being taught, to protect children's democratic right to freedom of religion, to foster an autonomy-enhancing understanding of faith, and to promote values such as concern for the salvation of persons, for stewardship of creation and for social justice.[30]

In 'Education in Religion and Spirituality from the Inside' the teacher assumes correctness of one religious/ spiritual worldview and actively encourages children to adopt that view. Here teachers are often expected to be believers in the religion themselves and tend to be personally committed to the religious perspective being taught. Furthermore, the religious/spiritual education offered is generally understood to be broader than the formal religious education curriculum: the worldview of the child is formed through the entire ethos of the school and the personal witness and commitment of the teacher. As John Sullivan explains:

> Faith schools provide a safe context for students and teachers to remain 'under the umbrella' of a particular living tradition, to spend an extended period of time thinking according to its conceptual categories, evaluating experiences from its vantage point, looking out at the world from a particular angle, familiarising themselves with a particular story, internalising a set of practices, rehearsing the rules of belonging to a particular community, letting the 'tools' or 'resources' provided by a religious way of life become, at least for a while, extensions of themselves in their attentiveness, experiences, judgements and decisions.[31]

Table 4 summaries the differences between two specific expressions of 'Education in Religion and Spirituality from the Outside' and 'Education in Religion and Spirituality from the Inside'. 'Education in Religion and Spirituality from the Outside' is exemplified in the liberal model of religious education.[32] 'Education in Religion and Spirituality from the Inside' is exemplified in the Catholic model of religious education.

Table 4: Exemplars of the Two Types of Religious Education

Approach to Religious Education	Outsider (Liberal)	Insider (Catholic)
Metaphysical worldview	Secular. Belief in God/Mystery/ the Sacred is possible, valid, but an option.	Faith perspective: the existence of God is assumed. God is the foundation of all reality.
View of the learner	Person understood in terms of their relationship with the natural order. Learner is critical questioner and reflective searcher.	Person understood in terms of their relationship with God. Learner is one who makes a free and rational response to Revelation.
Possible views of religion	Western representations of religion rooted in Enlightenment thought and based on disciplines such as anthropology, sociology, history, philosophy and psychology. Religion as a gift to the pupils' spiritual and ethical imagination and a resource for their search for meaning and values. Liberal protestant theological approach to religion. (Religious experience is fundamental for understanding religion; religions are different but complementary expressions of the divine.)	Religion as a revealed source of graced transformation. Religion as a way of living and as a path to salvation. Emphasis on Catholic theological approaches to religion, though other disciplines (anthropology, sociology, history, philosophy and psychology) may also be drawn upon. Participation in religious language and practices, and the holding of certain beliefs, are fundamental to an understanding of religion.

Approaches to Religious Education

Approach to Religious Education	Outsider (Liberal)	Insider (Catholic)
Locus for religion and spirituality	The private individual. Religion/spirituality concerned mainly with inner, private experience. Religion restricted to a special realm in life (v. the secular realm).	The person-in-community. Religion concerned with inner experience and with public knowledge and action. Religion as comprehensive, referring to every moment of life.
Mode of approach	Reason seeking an understanding of faith. Enlightenment approach to religion; observing religions from an 'impartial', external standpoint. Religion is instrumentalised so that the experience and development of the self of the learner are prioritised. Emphasis on skills and attitudes needed for living with religious diversity in society.	Faith seeking understanding. Revelation is primary; learner's experience and reason are brought into dialogue with it. Learner reflects critically and creatively on a lived Christian faith. Emphasis on celebration of and participation in a lived experience of the Divine.
Goal	Knowledge, understanding and appreciation of religion; cultural understanding. Independent and autonomous thought in relation to religion.	Religious understanding, religious and moral identity formation, internal reflective belief and practice. Learning a way of life that leads to salvation.

Approach to Religious Education	Outsider (Liberal)	Insider (Catholic)
Goal (contd.)	Clarification of views and self-identity, meaning-making. Tolerance and respect. Reduction of religious and racial prejudice, inter-religious harmony. Democratic citizenship. Social cohesion.	Cultivating a disposition of receptivity to the Mystery of God. Knowledge and appreciation of own religion and the religions and worldviews of others. Contributing to citizenship, inter-religious harmony and the common good via commitment to the Catholic religion.
Epistemology (How do we come to know in the domain of religion?)	May favour a non-realist approach to religion. Favours the students' horizon of meaning and the horizon of meaning of the discipline chosen to study religion (sociology, psychology, anthropology, etc.). Emphasis on rational thought, critical evaluation and skills of self-determination. May place the truth of religion(s) in question or avoid the question of truth. Knowledge through reason and/or various methods which give students an 'experience' of religion (e.g. meditation).	Realist approach to religion. Catholic religion is seen as true. Favours the horizon of meaning contained in the Catholic religion. Focus on truth and revelation, responding to God. Emphasis on symbolic and mystical imagination as well as critical reflection. Rationality informed by revelation. Reason illumined by faith. Students invited to experience the presence of God using language and practices particular to Catholicism (e.g. Christian meditation).

Approach to Religious Education	Outsider (Liberal)	Insider (Catholic)
Teaching posture	'Impartiality', 'fairness' and/'epistemological openness'. Promotes a secular liberal view of religion. 'Sceptical neutrality of reason in relation to religion'.[33]	Evangelical, positively disposed toward the Catholic religion. Promotes particular theological approaches to the Catholic faith.

Strengths and weaknesses of the approaches

What follows is a generalised attempt to summarise the current debate on the possible strengths and weaknesses of both the 'insider' and 'outsider' approaches to religious education. This is presented with some caution because there is always a danger of polarising approaches without recognising that they have much in common. Note also that this discussion is not intended to address specific religious education curricula currently being taught in Irish schools. (Every model of religious education should be assessed on its own merits, in the particular socio-cultural context in which it is being used). Rather, the goal is to alert readers to some of the typical arguments found in the literature in support of or criticising the two idealised approaches outlined above. Of course, no actual curriculum of religious education will correspond to all of the strengths and weaknesses outlined here. Furthermore, it is important to note that many of the claims below have not been proven by empirical research. (This is why the qualifier 'may' is used before each and every statement.) With that caveat in mind, it is nevertheless hoped that readers will be prompted to begin to critically examine actual religious education practices in their own context.

Possible strengths of 'outsider' approaches
'Outsider approaches' may:

» Treat religions and other stances for living fairly, respecting the uniqueness of each perspective and encouraging expression of a diversity of religious and spiritual belief and practice. As such, these approaches give recognition to some of the religions that are practised in society and in this way some religious children may feel that their identity is being affirmed. Children whose religions are included in the programme should have a positive experience in seeing that their religion and its distinctive contribution to society is recognised and respected.[34]

» Help to prevent religious indifference and relativism, religious prejudice, religious fundamentalism, racism, hatred and ignorance of religion when accurate descriptions of religions are presented, when 'crude caricatures and distorted accounts' of religious phenomena are challenged and when children are invited to understand and appreciate the logic and practice of religion.[35]

» Be very inclusive in that most children in the school may choose to participate in the same programme. No religion is singled out as being of more importance than any other and children may experience a freedom to discuss religious matters with other children who have differing life commitments to their own.

» Enable the development of understanding, respect, tolerance and openness in relation to religious and spiritual matters. Students may be enabled to develop a readiness for dialogue with people who do not share their worldview and an appreciation of religious, spiritual and ethical diversity in general. They may be invited to go beyond mere tolerance of others to engage in authentic dialogue and the search for common ethical values.

» Enable children to appreciate the religious way of life as an alternative to non-religious approaches. This is particularly important for children who are not being raised in a particular religion by their parents. The opportunity to explore the domain of religion in school may help ensure that children's autonomy is enhanced and that their rights to a basic religious education are honoured.[36]

» Enable students to appreciate the contribution made by religious people to Irish society and to the wider world. It is very important that children understand the important contribution of religious adherents, and of those committed to other life stances, to life in the public square. Genuine pluralism requires that people not leave their most cherished beliefs and commitments behind them when they enter public life. On the contrary, people who have a strong religious or ethical identity bring a richness to public discourse that is crucial for the health of liberal democracies.

» Focus on the children as learners and on what they can learn *from* religion(s) for their own moral, spiritual and religious development. Rather than simply teaching children *about* religions, a genuine attempt may be made to enable students to draw wisdom for their spiritual, moral and religious lives from the religions and other stances for living presented.

» Enjoy a relative freedom from the oversight of religious leaders and authorities in their presentation of religions in education and may therefore be more likely to be innovative in the pedagogical theories and approaches adopted.

Possible strengths of 'insider' approaches

'Insider approaches' may:

» Stay true to the nature of religion as something that is lived by people in community. As such they enable children to experience a quality of understanding which can only be achieved by being involved and engaged in a religion. Thus, for example, children come to understand what it means to be a Christian by practising Christian faith, a Muslim by practising Islam, a Jew by practising Judaism, etc.

» Honour the value of learning about that which is outside the subjectivity of the learner and avoid reducing learning to the experience and development of the self of the learner. Such learning involves the development of ways of knowing and a possible transformation of consciousness that would not be possible in 'outside' approaches.[37]

» Enable children to receive systematic, in-depth religious education in their own religion in a manner which respects their right to develop a strong worldview. As Terence McLaughlin argues, religious parents can provide a 'substantive religious upbringing' for their children which helps provide some balance to the formative influences of a secular culture that may be either indifferent to or hostile to religious faith.[38] Children of religious parents are enabled to have an adequate and critical understanding of their family's religion, so that they can make informed choices in their future as autonomous agents.[39] Ian MacMullen adds that the spiritual, religious and ethical formation children receive at home and in their community is reinforced, enabling them 'to build the psychological and cognitive resources needed to choose and lead a good life as an adult'.[40]

» Enable children to develop a rooted religious faith which empowers them to engage creatively, respectfully and constructively with difference. This is the argument that people who are religiously educated in the richness of their own religion may well be in the best position to have a genuine appreciation of the religions of others. One reason for this, as Alexander and McLaughlin explain, is that, because students are offered 'sustained and coherent exposure to the underlying philosophical assumptions' of one religious tradition, they may thereby be better placed to make judgements about the nature of the kinds of philosophical assumptions relevant to the religious and spiritual domains as a whole'.[41]

» Respect the fact that it is difficult if not impossible to educate religious children morally apart from their religion. Religious people tend to respond to something beyond the self as a basis for their moral life. For many religious people, for example, God is the reference point for their entire moral code and moral life is life lived with a consciousness of the person's relationship to the Divine. God is the criterion for a good human life and moral life often includes obedience to the commandments or moral precepts which are contained in sacred texts and are considered, by believers, to be revealed by God. Sacred scripture is a primary source for the moral education of Christians, for example, just as the Quran holds a preeminent place in the moral education of Muslims. Furthermore, there are intimate connections between religious convictions, moral reflection and action, and spiritual and ritual practices in religions. Religious education from the inside provides the context where children can reflect on their moral experiences, make moral judgements and respond morally in light of their religious faith.

» Be personally enriching and rewarding for teachers who are enabled to integrate their own spiritual path with their work as a teacher. As we noted in Chapter Three, an acknowledgement of the Divine (God) and the experience of dependence on something beyond the self does not merely influence the inner or private life of religious persons. Religion shapes all of their decisions, including their choice of work, the way they approach their work, the values that guide their interaction with work colleagues, the goals they aspire to in the workplace and the ultimate meaning they ascribe to what they do. Thus for example, Catholic teachers are invited to see religious education as part of their vocation to play a unique part in the fulfilment of God's purposes in the world.

Possible weaknesses of 'outsider' approaches
'Outsider approaches' may:
» Not represent the nature of religion and of what it means to be religious correctly or fairly. For example, religions may be portrayed as cultural artefacts, as 'equal and complementary paths to the Sacred' or as 'systems of belief'. As William Kay notes, religions can be thought of as

> belief systems without any apparent understanding of the complexity of these systems, their aesthetic implications, the sense of community engendered by religion, the emotional and ritual aspect of religion and the extensive moral corollaries that flow out of most religious traditions. By conceptualising religions as systems of belief, religions are shorn of their vital characteristics, decontextualised and reduced to skeletons.[42]

Equally, religious traditions and spiritual perspectives may be presented in a superficial and external manner, independently of actual religious and spiritual practice in a particular society and to the neglect of the spiritual and experiential dimension that provides the motivation for religious belief and practice.[43] As L. Philip Barnes explains, such approaches can be perceived by parents as hostile to their children's 'orthodox' religious convictions because they misrepresent their actual religious commitments.[44] In this respect, Terrence Merrigan warns that religions are complex multifaceted living traditions which cannot be understood without recourse to interpretations of the tradition offered by adherents of that tradition.[45]

» Present religions in a monolithic fashion, thus failing to represent the complexity within religions and among religions.[46] Lane expresses concern that, when religions are looked at from the perspective of secular reason, it 'may reduce the strangeness, difference and otherness that religion brings'.[47] Further, Lane notes:

> Education only *about* religion is premised on an enlightenment understanding of religion which neglects the diversity, difference and otherness which exists within religions and between religions. Neglect of these particular dimensions within religions and between religions forgets what is at the core of many religions, namely the existential, experiential, interpretive, affective, aesthetic and revelatory dimensions of religions.[48]

» Not address some of the fundamental issues of truth and commitment at stake in religion. For example, the phenomenological, the experiential and the ethnographic approaches focus on religious believers as people who do and believe certain things. The truth or otherwise of what they believe may not be addressed. Thus, McLoughlin and Alexander warn of the danger of 'distortive mishandling by teachers of underlying philosophical questions' relevant to religions leading to the possibility that students may be given the impression that 'relativism in its various forms is an appropriate (or inevitable) perspective to take toward the possibility and nature of "truth" in the religious and spiritual domains'.[49] In a similar vein, Barnes argues that phenomenological and liberal approaches fail to make pupils aware of the contested nature of religion and therefore fail to introduce students to 'the skills and considerations that are relevant to the assessment of religion and religious phenomena'.[50]

» Give tacit support to secularism and to moral and religious relativism. Gavin D'Costa has argued that, when judgements about religions can only be made from a secular, non-religious position so that no one religion is privileged, 'secular values and judgements are promoted in the process of evaluation'.[51] Other commentators have argued that, when children are not invited to engage in any particular religion or tradition of human self-understanding at a deep level, the school may give tacit support to a form of religious relativism.[52] This is a real danger when teachers inculcate in pupils the liberal conviction that the different religions are equal and complementary paths to salvation, that religious teachings give access to the same truth or that spiritualities promoted through different traditions are universal and common to all humanity.[53] The modern liberal Protestant thesis on the basic unity of religions is only one of a spectrum of theological possibilities and would be contested by many religious persons.[54]

» Reduce religion to the experience of the learner. When religion is seen merely as something which helps pupils to identify and reflect on their own search for meaning, the spiritual dimension of religion which calls for human transformation in the context of human responses to the transcendent/divine may be inadvertently downplayed. As Lane notes, some outside approaches emphasise construction 'at the expense of discovery, and openness to the strangeness, difference and otherness that religion brings'.[55] As a corollary of this, Sullivan argues that 'the authenticity of learners is privileged over the authority of the object of study ... This distorts the nature of at least some religions – Judaism, Christianity and Islam – as obedient responses to the prevenient address to us by God, and as wholehearted participation in a faith community'.[56] Furthermore, as Barnes notes, when teachers assume that the locus for both religion and spirituality is the private individual, this diminishes the role of sacred writings and religious authorities in the process by which a person's experience is structured and conditioned.[57]

» Overemphasise the role of conceptual knowledge and critical rationality in religious education when it is assumed that the aim is for students to acquire the skills and knowledge necessary for judging the value of religions for themselves. When the educational goal is understood in this fashion, it may convey the idea that religious faith is an intellectual proposal rather than a dynamism which involves cognitive, affective and behavioural dimensions. This belies the nature of religious understanding which is more an affective, behavioural mode of knowing than a rational choice. At worst, as Penny Thompson warns, there is a danger that students would get the impression that being religious is about making 'an arbitrary choice based on nothing more than some subjective preference'.[58]

» Instrumentalise the study of religion such that the unique contribution of religion to a person's education is forgotten. For example, when the primary purpose of religious education is understood in terms of what it contributes to the social or political aims of education, teaching for tolerance, respect and inter-religious harmony in society takes precedence over the intrinsic value of spiritual, moral and religious development and hence of being religiously educated in itself. Similarly, Clive Erricker has warned that educators may instrumentalise religion when they borrow from religious practices, rituals, symbolism and metaphors to enhance students' personal or spiritual development with no intention to engage with religions per se.[59] Learning *from* religion in the context of students' own search for meaning replaces any real attempt to learn *about* religion or to enter *into* religion in any other way.

» Not achieve the goals of tolerance and respect. A number of commentators have questioned whether religious education from the outside can achieve the lofty political goals increasingly assigned to it, given that, in most school settings, children receive one or two hours' religious education per week. Both Liam Gearon and L. Philip Barnes point out that we simply do not know whether multi-faith religious education actually contributes to social cohesion and develops respect and tolerance in pupils for those who espouse different values.[60] At present, Barres notes, 'there is no empirical evidence to substantiate a positive connection between multi-faith religious education and respectful attitudes towards members of minority religions and cultures'. There is, he says, some empirical evidence to show that teaching *about* religion has failed to promote tolerance of and respect for other religions.[61] Barnes suggests that some representations of religion in British religious education are 'conceptually ill-equipped to develop respect for difference', while Brenda Watson claims that neutral presentations of religious phenomena actually lead to religious indifference.[62]

Possible Weaknesses of 'insider approaches'
'Insider approaches' may:
» Place more emphasis on how education serves religious formation into particular religious traditions than how religion fits with the goals of education in liberal democratic societies. As a result, there is a danger that these approaches are too transmissive, with limited opportunities for openness, critical enquiry, and freedom. As Clive Erricker points out, when it is assumed that children will always learn *from* religion, the emphasis is on affirming religion's value, with the result that the harmful effects of religion tend to be downplayed.[63] If children are not invited to use their reason in relation to their own religion it may encourage parochialism, fideism, fundamentalism, sectarianism and uncritical socialisation. While none of these outcomes are inherent to faith-based education, they may result when faith-based education is taught with insufficient attention paid to contemporary educational theory, to the need for critical reason and to the ways young children learn.
» Treat children as objects of study rather than doing justice to children's moral, spiritual and theological potentialities. The content of the traditional religious texts (Catechism,

Quran, Bible, etc.) may be over-emphasised, leading to a neglect of children's own theological and existential questions. For example, Sullivan warns of the danger of Catholic educational approaches that treat the 'external, objective, institutional and hierarchical dimensions of the Church as if they include without remainder and must totally dominate the internal, subjective, personal and community dimensions'.[64] This may lead to curricular approaches where 'the objective and institutional pole' of Catholicism subsumes 'the subjective and personal pole' rather than relating to it in a more reciprocal manner.[65] Advocates of some inside approaches are uncomfortable with pluralism and often call for greater uniformity in language, educational methodologies and practice than is necessary for healthy religious learning.

» Fail to significantly distinguish religious education practices suited to the private sphere (home, mosque, synagogue, parish, etc.) from those which are appropriate to the academic discipline of religious education carried out in the public space. Clearly, children engaging in faith-based religious education in contemporary liberal societies come from a range of familial and social backgrounds, with varying levels of commitment to the religion in question. Programmes which require a high level of religious piety from students could be charged with being inauthentic and disrespectful to children when their real capacities for religious understanding and commitment are ignored. When teachers and curriculum leaders do not pay enough attention to the cultural reality in which religious education is carried out, and when assumptions of faith commitment are made that are unfounded in reality, it leads to inauthentic teaching and flawed educational materials.

» Assume a high level of uniformity in the way in which the religion in question is understood and practised in a particular society. Religious educators may give students the impression that religious adherents are completely united in thought and practice. Diversity and controversy within the religion being taught is ignored. A corollary to this is when the cognitive aspects of a religious faith – its beliefs – become divorced from how those beliefs are articulated and lived out in communities and particular cultures. The attempt is then made to impose one culturally limited language of religious belief on the whole community, with no awareness of the inculturated nature of each and every naming of religious doctrine. When this happens, curriculum and programme writers may become stifled by a kind of 'policing of the tradition' by religious leaders or self-appointed religious guardians. This may prevent educators from developing culturally adapted programmes with realistic educational goals.

» Limit exposure to differing religious and spiritual traditions, so that students are not prepared for meaningful dialogues with people who do not share their own life stance. Some 'inside' approaches may not pay enough attention to inter-religious education and the need to learn the public language of religion in a liberal democratic state. When this happens, there may be a danger that students would develop prejudiced or stereotyped views about other religious and spiritual paths. In some religious groups there may also be a resistance to those who seek to articulate the wisdom of a religious tradition in language that respects the needs and sensibilities of those outside the religious tradition who are open to dialogue.

» Be based on unfounded assumptions about the personal commitment and religious literacy of the teacher. Many faith-based approaches require a high level of commitment on the part of the teacher to the religion in question. Teachers may experience little recognition (by religious stakeholders, boards of management and parents) that the art of religious living has become very complex in our globalised world and that they too are on a spiritual journey which involves, alternately, attitudes of commitment, questioning and even lack of belief.

Conclusion

It is important for religious educators to be clear about the particular perspective (secular or faith-based) from which children will be asked to examine the domain of religion in religious education. It is also important to acknowledge that different approaches to religious education have merit in differing types of schools. Rather than polarising approaches it is helpful to examine the strengths and weaknesses of actual practices of religious education in the diverse schools you encounter.

All forms of religious and spiritual education should educate children towards/for forms of religious, spiritual or ethical identity that are simultaneously committed and open, rooted and adaptive – that is, forms of religious education that allow young children to begin to develop a deep appreciation and understanding of their own religion or life stance, but which also encourage engagement with people of differing religious faiths and other stances for living.[66] Ideally, all children should be educated in ways conducive to the development of healthy spiritual or religious identities and to healthy engagement with religious and spiritual pluralism, regardless of the schooling type they attend. Finally, all approaches to religious education should be culturally appropriate and educationally sound, while aiming to be as true as possible to the nature of religion as experienced and understood by the children with whom those types of religious education are carried out.

Questions for reflection

» What kind of learning in spirituality and religion is possible in a non-denominational/multi-denominational school? What kind of learning is possible in a denominational school?

» What difference does personal and family commitment make to the kind of understanding in religion children might achieve at school?

» What might *both* types of religious education contribute to the education of children as citizens of Ireland? What have they got in common?

» Discuss the challenges for you in teaching the two types of religious education outlined. Can you add to the lists of strengths and weaknesses outlined above? Do you agree/disagree with any?

» How can a commitment to children's spiritual, moral and religious development be balanced with the need to learn to live together with people of differing religions and life stances?

Supplementary reading

» Hanan Alexander and Terence H. McLaughlin, 'Education in Religion and Spirituality', in N. Blake, P. Smeyers, R. Smith and P. Standish (eds), *The Blackwell Guide to the Philosophy of Education* (Oxford: Blackwell, 2003), 356–73.

» William K. Kay, 'Philosophical Approaches to the Teaching of Religion in Schools', in Marian De Souza et al. (eds), *International Handbook of the Religious, Moral and Spiritual Dimensions in Education* (Dordrecht: Springer, 2006) 559–766.

» Philip L. Barnes, *Education, Religion and Diversity* (London: Routledge, 2014), for a critical analysis of the commitments and axioms of the phenomenological, experiential, liberal and post-modern models of religious education in Britain.

» Gareth Byrne and Patricia Kieran (eds), *Toward Mutual Ground: Pluralism, Religious Education and Diversity in Irish Schools* (Dublin: Columba, 2013). Chps. 1, 2, 4, and 6.

Endnotes

1. OSCE, *The Toledo guiding principles on teaching about religions and beliefs in public schools* (Warsaw: Organisation for Security and Co-operation in Europe, Office For Democratic Institutions and Human Rights), 69, found at http://www.osce.org/item/28314.html.

2. Clive Erricker, *Religious Education: a conceptual and interdisciplinary approach for secondary level* (London: Routledge, 2012), 9.

3. Michael Grimmitt, 'The Captivity and Liberation of Religious Education and the Meaning and Significance of Pedagogy' in Michael Grimmitt (ed), *Pedagogies of Religious Education* (Great Wakering, Essex: McCrimmons, 2000), 17.

4. Hanan Alexander and Terence H. McLaughlin, 'Education in Religion and Spirituality' in N. Blake, P. Smeyers, R. Smith and P. Standish (eds), *The Blackwell Guide to the Philosophy of Education* (Oxford: Blackwell, 2003), 356–73.

5. Andrew McGrady, 'Teaching Religion' in Gareth Byrne and Patricia Kieran (eds), *Toward Mutual Ground: Pluralism, Religious Education and Diversity in Irish Schools* (Dublin: Columba Press, 2013), 83.

6. For the way in which the political interest manifest in religion has impacted on secular forms of religious education in Western liberal democracies, see Liam Gearon, *MasterClass in Religious Education: Transforming Teaching and Learning* (London: Bloomsbury, 2013).

7. Lieven Boeve, 'Religious Education in a post-secular and post-Christian context', *Journal of Beliefs & Values* (2012), 33(2): 147.

8. On how different approaches to the study of religion lead to differing pedagogies of religious education, see Erricker, ibid., Chapter 3.

9. Robert Jackson, *Rethinking Religious Education and Plurality: Issues in Diversity and Pedagogy* (London: RoutledgeFalmer, 2004), 165.

10. Alexander and McLaughlin, ibid., 364.

11. Alexander and McLaughlin, ibid., 361.

12. Note the concepts of learning *about* religion and *from* religion were first introduced by Michael Grimmitt and Garth Read in 1975. Michael Grimmitt and Garth Read, Teaching Christianity in RE (Great Wakering, Essex: Mayhew, 1975). The definitive statement is found in Grimmitt's *Religious Education and Human Development* (Great Wakering, Essex: McCrimmon Publishing, 1987), 224–66.
13. Dermot A Lane, *Religion and Education: re-imagining the relationship* (Dublin: Veritas, 2013), 26–7.
14. For the distinction between healthy secularism and ideological secularism see Lane, ibid., 40. Referring to these approaches, Robert Jackson argues: 'If they are *secular*, then they are so only in the sense used in the Indian constitution which, like article 18 of the *Universal Declaration of Human Rights* and other human rights codes is intended as a guarantee of freedom of religion or belief'. Robert Jackson, ibid., 165.
15. It is becoming increasingly common for social scientists and commentators to make a distinction between procedural secularism and programmatic secularism. See Rowan Williams, 'Secularism, Faith and Freedom', *Faith in the Public Square* (London: Bloomsbury, 2012), 23–36. See glossary.
16. Note however that this is not true of all approaches. Robert Jackson's interpretive approach, for example, requires that the teacher teach with 'impartiality' which, he claims, is not the same as 'neutrality'. Teachers can bring their own belief commitments into the classroom as resources but they must be able to 'countenance rival conclusions as well as those to which they are personally attached and know how and when to contain their commitments and how to present material from a religious tradition from the point of view of an adherent'. Robert Jackson, *Religious Education: an Interpretive Approach* (London: Hodder & Stoughton, 1997), 136.
17. Boeve, ibid., 148.
18. Alexander and McLaughlin, ibid., 363
19. John Sullivan 'Dismembering and Remembering Religious Education', in Marius Felderhof, Penny Thompson and David Torevell (eds), *Inspiring Faith in Schools* (Hampshire: Ashgate, 2007), 129–30.
20. Jackson, *Rethinking*, 165.
21. Grimmitt, ibid., 225.
22. Lane, ibid., 27.
23. Sandra Cullen, 'Toward an Appropriate Religious Education for Future Teachers of Religious Education' (2013), Mater Dei Institute of Education, Dublin City University, unpublished doctoral thesis, 110.
24. John Sullivan, 'Faith Schools: a culture within a culture in a changing world', in M. de Souza et al. (eds), *International Handbook of the Religious, Moral and Spiritual Dimensions in Education* (Dordrecht: Springer, 2006), 940.
25. Sullivan, 'Dismembering and Remembering Religious Education', in Marius Felderhof et al. (eds), ibid., 129.
26. Alexander and McLaughlin, ibid., 369.
27. Alexander and McLaughlin, ibid., 361. For International instruments of human rights which uphold the right of parents to choose the kind of education that shall be given to their children, see The Universal Declaration of Human Rights (1948) (Art. 26.3), The United Nations International Covenant on Economic, Social and Cultural Rights (1966) (Art. 13.3) and The European Convention on Human Rights (Protocol 1, Art. 2). This right is established in Article 42 of the Irish Constitution (1937).

28. Peter Schreiner, 'Different Approaches – Common Aims? Current Developments in Religious Education in Europe', in Peter Schreiner, Hans Spinder, Jeremy Taylor and Wim Westerman (eds), *Committed to Europe's Future: contributions from Education and Religious Education: a Reader* (Münster: Comenius Institute, 2002), 97.
29. Friedrich Schweitzer, 'Children's Right to Religion and Spirituality: Legal, Educational and Practical Perspectives', in *British Journal of Religious Education* (2005) 27: 103–113.
30. On faith-based education that enhances autonomy, see T. H. McLoughlin, 'Parental rights and the religious upbringing of children', *Journal of Philosophy of Education* (1984), 18(1): 75–83.
31. John Sullivan, 'Faith Schools: a culture within a culture in a changing world', in de Souza et al. (eds), ibid., 941.
32. The central beliefs and commitments of the liberal model of religious education are outlined by Philip L. Barnes in *Education, Religion and Diversity*, Chapter 9.
33. Gearon, ibid., 143.
34. L. Philip Barnes, 'Religious Education and the Misrepresentation of Religion' in Felderhof et al. (eds), ibid., 85.
35. Barnes, ibid., 85.
36. On the implications of the 1989 Convention on the Rights of the Child for religious education see O. Jawoniyi, 'Children's Rights and Religious Education in State Funded Schools: an International Human Rights Perspective', *International Journal of Human Rights* (2012), 16(2): 337–57.
37. Lane, ibid., 27.
38. T. H. McLaughlin, 'Religion, upbringing and liberal values: a rejoinder to Eamonn Callan', *Journal of Philosophy of Education* (1985), 19(1): 119–27.
39. Various authors argue some version of what Eamonn Callan calls the 'initiation thesis'. The classic statement of the argument was made by Terence McLaughlin. See T. H. McLaughlin, 'Religion, upbringing and liberal values: a rejoinder to Eamonn Callan', 119–27.
40. Ian McMullen, 'Education for Autonomy: the Role of Religious Elementary Schools, *Journal of Philosophy of Education*(2004), 38(4): 603.
41. Alexander and McLaughlin, ibid., 370.
42. William K. Kay, 'Philosophical Approaches to the Teaching of Religion in Schools', in M. de Souza et al. (eds.), ibid., 567. See also L. Philip Barnes, 'Religious Education and the Misrepresentation of Religion', 75–85.
43. This is one of the most common criticisms of the phenomenological approach which is concerned with describing observable phenomena of religions and the religious practices of adherents. (Barnes, *Education, Religion and Diversity*, 105.) Barnes also notes that many faith community members in Britain are concerned about how their faith is represented and treated in schools. Barnes, 'Religious Education and the Misrepresentation of Religion', 76, 83.
44. L. Philip Barnes, *Education, Religion and Diversity*, 2, 18, 157.
45. Terrence Merrigan, 'Religion, Education and the Appeal to Plurality: Theological Considerations on the Contemporary European Context' in Byrne and Kieran (eds), ibid., 58.
46. Erricker, ibid., 46.
47. Lane, ibid., 17.
48. Lane, ibid., 24.
49. Alexander and McLaughlin, ibid., 367.
50. Barnes, 'Religious Education and the Misrepresentation of Religion', 77.
51. Gavin D'Costa, 'Catholicism, Religious Pluralism and Education for the Common Good', in Byrne and Kieran (eds), ibid., 115.

52. See Rik Van Nieuwenhove, 'Is there any Mutual Ground? Some Critical Remarks on Pluralism and Non-Denominationalism' in Gareth Byrne and Patricia Kieran (eds), ibid., 196–7. Alexander and McLaughlin, ibid., 368. J. Mark Halstead, 'In Defence of Faith Schools' in Graham Haydon (ed.), *Faith in Education* (London: Institute of Education, University of London, 2009), 64. On the difficulties of a relativistic approach to pluralism, see Congregation for Catholic Education, *Educating to Intercultural Dialogue in Catholic Schools: Living in Harmony for a Civilization of Love*, 2013, nos. 22–3.

53. This is the underlying theological commitment of the liberal model of religious education. See Barnes, *Education, Religion and Diversity*, Chapters 6–10 for a comprehensive critique of the philosophical and theological assumptions underpinning phenomenological, experiential and liberal approaches to religious education. See also Erricker, ibid., 55.

54. Of course, approaches 'from the outside' which make these assumptions *will* be congenial to the cultural beliefs and values of many parents of secular conviction, humanists, cultural liberals and religious relativists.

55. Lane, ibid., 17.

56. Sullivan, 'Dismembering and Remembering Religious Education', in Felderfhof et al. (eds), ibid., 129–30.

57. Barnes, *Education, Religion and Diversity*, 108.

58. Penny Thompson, 'Religious education from Spens to Swann', in Felderhof et al (eds), ibid., 73.

59. Erricker, ibid., 34.

60. Barnes presents some empirical evidence and research that touches on this question in Barnes, *Education, Religion and Diversity*, 19–21. Gearon notes that we have no models of assessment for the grandiose political goals ascribed to some 'outside' approaches. He points to 'a more fundamental difficulty in conceptualizing in psychological, political or socio-cultural terms how success might be envisaged', Gearon, ibid., 141.

61. Barnes 'Religious Education and the Misrepresentation of Religion', 76. Lane, ibid., 24. L. Philip Barnes argues that the liberal model of religious education is 'conceptually incapable of challenging intolerance' in *Education, Religion and Diversity*, Chapter 10. In Chapter 12 he outlines the weakness of Robert Jackson's interpretive approach in challenging cultural and religious prejudice. Lane cites John Keast, who points out that 'learning about religion is insufficient in itself to produce the kind of respectful attitudes that community and school cohesion requires in a multifaith society'. John Keast, 'Use of "Distancing" and "Simulation"' in *Religious Diversity and Intercultural Education: a Reference Book for Schools* (Council of Europe Publishing, 2007), 62. See also Gearon, ibid., 34.

62. L. P. Barnes, 'World Religions in British Religious Education: Critical Reflections and Positive Conclusions', *Journal of Religious Education* (2003), 51(2): 34–41, 76; Brenda Watson, *The Effective Teaching of Religious Education* (London: Longman, 1993), 43–6, as cited in Barnes, 'World Religions', 76.

63. Erricker, ibid., 8.

64. John Sullivan, *Catholic Education: Distinctive and Inclusive* (Dordrecht: Springer, 2001), 39

65. Sullivan, ibid., 42–3. These concerns are echoed in Pope Francis' Apostolic Exhortation, *Evangelii Gaudium* (The Joy of the Gospel), (Dublin: Veritas, 2013), nos. 27, 35, 41, 45.

66. See Mary. C. Boys and Sara S. Lee, *Christians and Jews in dialogue: learning in the presence of the other* (Woodstock, ON: Skylight Paths, 2006).

SECTION THREE
UNDERSTANDING CATHOLIC PRIMARY RELIGIOUS EDUCATION

CHAPTER FIVE
RELIGIOUS EDUCATION IN CATHOLIC PRIMARY SCHOOLS

Being a Christian is not the result of an ethical choice or a lofty idea, but the encounter with an event, a person, which gives life a new horizon and a decisive direction.[1]

POPE BENEDICT XVI

A strong religious belief is not an obstacle to being tolerant; on the contrary, it can be the precondition of a tolerance that respects the other person, including what the other person believes.[2]

GABRIEL MORAN

CATHOLIC PRIMARY RELIGIOUS EDUCATION INVOLVES INVITING children to explore and understand how to live a Christian way of life. It introduces children to the Christian religious tradition and invites them to learn what it means to have a personal faith relationship with Jesus Christ. This form of religious education supports the development of a distinctive religious identity in the context of diversity – one that is simultaneously distinctive and inclusive, rooted and open, committed and tolerant, receptive and enquiring. Catholic religious education aims to protect children's religious freedom and to promote critical understanding of their religious faith. As such it rejects transmissive or 'banking' models of education in favour of child-centred approaches favouring dialogue, critical enquiry, openness, creativity, imagination, language development, play and engagement with children's lived experience of religion in contemporary society.

Catholic primary religious education lays the foundations for religious education at secondary level and beyond. As such, it is best understood as a first step on a *life-long* journey of continuing spiritual, moral and religious development. At primary level, therefore, teachers will be attentive to the developmental stage, interests, language, aptitudes, spiritual maturity and diverse cultural backgrounds of children.[3] Ultimately, the religiously educated Catholic will be a person who understands, appreciates and lives her own faith, while being capable of critical reflection on that faith. She will be capable of encounter and dialogue with people of other worldviews and will have a genuine appreciation and empathetic understanding of other religious ways.[4]

Education and theology in dialogue

Catholic religious education draws on the disciplines of theology, religious studies and education for its underlying principles, theories and values.[5] While other approaches to religious education might invite students to examine religion from a secular position (phenomenological, sociological, historical, ethnographic), Catholic religious education presents religious concepts and practices from a Catholic insider's theological point of view.[6] Furthermore, while Catholic religious education utilises the best contemporary psychological and sociological perspectives on human development, it draws its particular understanding of the person and of personal development mainly from Christian theology. In other words, theology defines many of the Christian attributes, values, practices, moral actions, and types of consciousness and understanding that the Catholic religious education curriculum tries to promote.[7]

Two types of learning

Gabriel Moran, the eminent American religious education theorist, argues that the practice of religious education has two aspects or 'faces'. Religious education involves two types of learning: one focused on learning how to live a religious way of life, the other on learning for the sake of understanding.[8] Catholic primary religious education aspires to engage children in both of these types of learning. In other words, it incorporates what Jeff Astley calls a 'formation dimension' and a 'critical dimension'.[9] There should be a creative and interdependent relationship between these two aspects of religious education in Catholic primary schools.

Catholic Religious Education

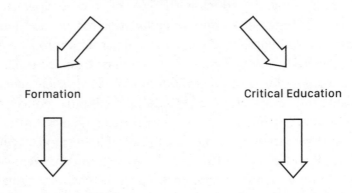

Formation   Critical Education

Religious Understanding   Understanding Religion

Formation

The first aim of Catholic religious education is to enable children to immerse themselves in Christian religious beliefs, practices and values, inviting them to live inside the Christian vision of the good life. This is formation or nurture. The goal, in the schooling context, is religious understanding and the promotion of belonging and commitment to the Catholic religious tradition and to the Church community.[10] Here the child is invited to acquire some of the knowledge, ways of knowing, feelings, attitudes, values, skills, behaviours and sensibilities that being Christian involves. Most importantly, at primary level, children learn what they need to live Christian spiritual lives *as children*. Therefore, all formation should be appropriate to the psychological and spiritual development of the young child.

Revelation: call and response

An appreciation of what Catholics mean by 'revelation'

and how human persons respond to 'revelation' is crucial for understanding the kind of religious formation that is proposed in Catholic schools. Catholics believe that there is an initiating agency, named God, who is independent of anything in our world, but which is revealed to us in experience, in history, in creation and in particular in the life, death and resurrection of Jesus Christ. The Second Vatican Council, in its document on revelation (*Dei Verbum*) underlined that revelation is essentially the personal self-communication of God to humankind through Jesus Christ.[11] In other words, God reveals Godself to us in Jesus. And what Jesus reveals is a God who is continually present to us in our own being, a God who promotes fullness of life for all people without discrimination, a God who has mercy and compassion, a God who has a preferential regard for the poor and the suffering. As such revelation is a gift freely given by God to which all persons are invited (but never forced) to respond. We can respond by accepting the gift of God's love and by freely choosing to trust, identify and move with the creative and redemptive action of God as it has shown itself to us in Jesus.

So the dynamic of Christian faith is all about God's loving call and our free response; the dynamic is not one of question and answer, not an intellectual choice between options, not an uncritical assent to a set of beliefs. Instead, when we respond in faith we are invited to a new way of being, a new way of experiencing the world and ourselves in it, a different level of consciousness, a new identity in relationship with Jesus Christ. In other words, being religious in a Catholic way is essentially about *experiencing* Jesus Christ at the heart of our own lives in such a way that everything we do is shaped and empowered by that encounter. Becoming Christian is about embarking on a journey of ongoing intellectual, moral and spiritual transformation, reordering our priorities and ways of valuing ourselves, other people and the world.

A unique way of knowing

If this is what Christian faith is, how do we teach it? The nature of Christian faith itself shapes the skills and 'ways of knowing' we utilise in our attempt to teach and understand it. But how do we come to 'know' and so *experience* Jesus Christ? What kind of knowing is engaged in by those who accept the Bible and Tradition as sources of revelation? What kind of knowing opens us up to a transformation of consciousness such that we begin to see differently and value differently in the world?

In our culture we are initiated into the belief that what counts for knowledge is the rational, abstract, value-neutral, apolitical, universal knowledge: so-called objective knowledge. This approach to knowledge assumes that only the methodological criteria of modern science and of analytic reason can be used to determine what can be classified as knowledge and knowing. Kate Siejk has explained that, in this approach to knowledge, 'value is assigned to objectivity and its defining features, while all of the characteristics traditionally associated with subjectivity (e.g. feeling, emotion, sensitivity, empathy) are denied worth'.[12] This is why it seems like common sense to some that children should only receive religious education in the shape of an 'objective', 'impartial' description of religions and beliefs. Such a proposal assumes that children can learn *about* something in an entirely abstract, objective manner, escaping any taint of bias, subjectivity or emotion.

Here the illusion is created that scientific knowledge and analytic reason are superior to any other form of knowing that children might possibly be invited to undertake.

The scientific method gives us access only to one domain of knowledge. Scientific method offers an account of human knowledge that is constructed from rationally decisive evidence: It cannot give us insight into the totality of human experience. There are other dimensions of knowing beyond that offered by science. These are the personal, the aesthetic, the interpretative and transcendent dimensions of knowing and understanding.[13] Many of the subjects on the primary school curriculum also invite children to engage in these kinds of knowing and religious education has much in common with subjects like art, drama, music and literacy. Catholic religious education enables children to come to 'know', not only physical or natural things, but also non-physical realities, such as God's Holy Spirit and their own souls. These are realities that cannot ultimately be proven by the methods of science. If they could be proven they would cease to be what they are. Nor can they be accessed through reason alone. Sometimes, coming to 'know' in the domain of religion involves transcending rational thought to experience the Divine in contemplation or meditation, for example.

So Catholic religious education represents the act of knowing quite differently to scientific objectivism. This is because, for the Catholic, the supernatural realm (the Divine) is real and can be known. Here, to know something is to know it in and through relationship in such a way that it can surprise and transform us. This has been described by Parker Palmer as a 'relational way of knowing', which requires that we practise knowing as a form of love and not as power.[14] As such, it allows for the 'otherness' of religion and guards against the human temptation to reduce the sacred or the Divine to reason, facts, logic and data. Catholic religious education invites us to see religion as a subject that calls us deeper into its wisdom, a subject that can never be reduced to logical abstractions, collections of data, rational certainties, or conclusions.

The cognitive, affective and behavioural dimensions of knowing in Christian faith

There are three dimensions or aspects of knowing in Christian faith that are taught in religious education. First, faith has a specific content, consisting of a body of knowledge which has been revealed and a religious tradition that is handed on in the Church. The distinctive beliefs and doctrines of Christian faith structure the personal experience of faith and are essential to it. Therefore, it is important that children are enabled to understand and explore Christian beliefs and teachings and to make judgements and decisions about how they affect their lives. This is the cognitive dimension to Christian faith.

However, our educational goals do not stop there. Christian faith is always a personal act, a process of developing a trusting *relationship* with God in Jesus Christ that is nurtured and realised in prayer and worship and in relationship with a Christian faith community. To trust in Jesus in this way and to enter into deeper relationships with others, requires that our feelings and emotions are engaged at a deep level. In this sense, Catholic religious education encourages children to develop certain spiritual attitudes (e.g. trust, awe, wonder, reverence, adoration, joy), virtues (e.g. faith, hope and love) and values (e.g. gratitude, forgiveness, compassion, mercy). This is the affective dimension of Christian faith.

Finally, there is a behavioural or action dimension to learning in Christian faith: one learns how to be Christian by carrying out Christian actions and learning Christian practices. Christian faith is essentially a following of Jesus, through loving God and loving one's neighbour as oneself. It is a way of *living* according to God's purposes in the world and it is only in doing God's will in the world that God is truly known. In sum, Catholic religious education invites children to learn how to *think* and to *feel* and to *act* religiously in community. The whole person is involved – cognition, feelings, attitudes, values, as well as actions, involvement and participation.[15]

Knowing and the curriculum

When religion is approached, not as an object to be controlled, not as a 'belief system', not as a set of interesting cultural practices or as a set of propositions to be believed in, but as a lived response to God's loving presence and action in people's lives, it changes the kinds of curricular activities that are valued: analysing and evaluating religion on our own terms will be important, but so too will be our capacity for receptivity, for learning the revealed content of Catholic faith and for encountering something that ultimately transcends rational categories and cannot be controlled by us.[16] Critical thought will be balanced with symbolic or metaphorical thinking, which draws on the imagination. Methods of worship and prayer, creative engagement with story and poetry, exploration of the silence that leads to listening to God, reflection on nature and on human experience, learning how to care for one another and the earth, will be just as important as problem solving, critical analysis and evaluation.[17]

Teaching metaphorical thinking

Much of the language used in the Christian religion is language used metaphorically. For example, metaphor is the principal means by which Christians speak about God. When we say Mother God, we mean God is *like* all the best characteristics of human mothers that we can think of, but God is not literally a woman. So too the ability to understand parables and much biblical material requires an ability to deal with metaphors and to think symbolically. For example, the parable of the Good Shepherd suggests to Christians that the experience of being cared for and loved by God is similar to the way a good shepherd cares for and loves his sheep. In this way, biblical metaphors and symbols evoke God's love and compassion and Jesus' vision of the Reign of God. Children begin to learn to think religiously by constructing or inheriting metaphors.[18] Symbolic thinking of this sort requires a particular educational approach.

Teaching through symbolic play and narrative

Young children's ability to understand religious metaphors and to engage in symbolic activity is nurtured best through symbolic play, poetry, narrative strategies and ritual activity. These activities invite children to encounter religious symbol and imagery on the level of their senses, enabling them to think symbolically in a concrete rather than in an abstract way. Play utilises a mode of knowing that is closer to artistic creativity than the kinds of intellectual problem-solving and theological reflection *about* God which require logical or abstract thought. It engages imagination and wonder to enable children to find the Christian meaning of their experiences *as children*. Examples of activities that engage children in creative religious play include storytelling and response, dramatic improvisation, modelling with clay, drawing, painting, weaving, dancing, being still, listening and responding to music and poetry, and developing rhymes, chants and songs. Children also learn how to engage with religious symbol through their participation in liturgy, both inside and outside the classroom.

Teaching through story is central to the religious education of young children. Jesus understood the power of images to challenge people's way of seeing reality and so he often chose to teach people in parables, ritual, images and metaphor. Through the vehicle of the parable he gave his listeners a glimpse of his experience of God, an experience which radically upturns one's ideas, perspectives, values, and way of living. Sacred Scripture helps nurture a distinctly Christian religious imagination, enabling children to see things differently from the ways to which they have become accustomed.

When children are taught through liturgy, sacred image, play, sacred story and parable they are being introduced to ways of knowing that go beyond what they can know through scientific language or in rational discourse. Ultimately children are invited to *experience* the sacred, and to open themselves to the possibility of being met by God. Further, the use of these creative activities enables children to develop varied expressions of loving response to God.

Critical education

The second aspect of Catholic religious education involves critical understanding of and debate about religion, both one's own and that of others. It includes ecumenical education and inter-religious learning. The goal here is understanding religion.[19] The word 'critical' means 'careful judgement and decision'. It means standing back, taking a second look at something, becoming aware of one's assumptions, prejudices and biases, and making a genuine attempt to discern the truth of what it is one is studying. Critical religious education should foster an open, critical consciousness in the learner. The ability to evaluate one's own religion includes critically assessing that which is taught in the light of one's own experiences and that of others, both in the past and in the present. Religious faith must stand up under the test of the truth of lived experience – of self, others and the world.

According to Moran, the critical dimension of religious education aim to enable students to understand and appreciate the place of religious experience, beliefs and practices in human life, and to learn to explore issues of religion in a critical and unbiased way.[20] The need to teach people to think critically about religion stems from the fact that people ought to be free to accept or reject what is taught in religion.[21] Furthermore, a critical approach to one's own religious tradition is an indispensable part of the process whereby people adopt a religious way of life as their own. As John Sullivan argues, critical openness *from* a religious tradition facilitates openness and inclusiveness.[22] Explaining the importance of questioning in faith-based religious education, he argues that:

A faith school should provide a safe place in which the religious tradition can be encountered, expressed, witnessed to and lived out, without embarrassment of undue self-consciousness. Yet, at the same time, it should also provide a safe space in which it is possible to question the meaning, significance, coherence, adequacy, comprehensiveness, consistency, relevance and applicability of the faith tradition and to compare its teachings and practices with those of other world-views, without this questioning being taken as necessarily an indication of lack of commitment, of weak faith, of disloyalty or of inadequate understanding.[23]

Critical openness in religious education should be informed by analysis and rational judgement which tends towards decision and commitment. It should encourage students, in the first place to make a judgement as to the truth of the religious ideas under discussion, critically comparing the wisdom offered by the religious tradition with the longings of their own hearts.[24] Then, it should enable students to discover, judge and decide how religious experience and insight impacts upon their way of living in the world. As Astley explains:

> Critical study of religion includes aspects of critical pedagogy in that it aims to maximise the intellectual autonomy, responsibility and accountability of learners, but it is not confined to it. Critical reason must be combined with developing capacities for positive insight and openness to the possibility of non-sensory knowledge. Therefore, it is a form of critical openness that leads to the decision to act for the good, rather than autonomous speculation that is the mark of the kind of education proposed here.[25]

Faith and reason

In the Catholic primary school, critical education means understanding and critically reflecting on the Christian religion in ways appropriate to the developing child's capacities. The Catholic tradition has a strong commitment to the place of reason in the process of coming to faith and is strongly opposed to indoctrination in any form.[26] As Dermot Lane explains, 'the act of faith is always a free act and if it loses that freedom, or if coercion is brought to bear, then it is no longer faith but some form of ideology'.[27] John Hull adds, 'Critical openness is a discipline which the Christian follows not in spite of his faith but because of it'.[28] The authors of the 1988 document from the Sacred Congregation for Catholic Education, *The Religious Dimension of Education in a Catholic School*, directed that:

> The religious freedom and the personal conscience of individual students and their families must be respected, and this freedom is explicitly recognised by the Church. On the other hand, a Catholic school cannot relinquish its own freedom to proclaim the Gospel and to offer a formation based on the values to be found in a Christian education; this is its right and its duty. To proclaim or to offer is not to impose, however; the latter suggests a moral violence which is strictly forbidden, both by the Gospel and by Church law.[29]

Formation vs critical education?

While it is important to introduce children to the skills of critical reflection at every age, there is probably a greater emphasis on formation and nurture at primary level, as children need to develop a solid worldview and system of values before they begin to critically evaluate that worldview. In this I would agree with Astley when he says that '[e]ducation in general – and Christian religious education in particular – should recognise that, logically and psychologically, the formation of a person's identity and worldview must happen before [critical analysis and evaluation of knowledge claims] develops'.[30]

In other words, the basis for autonomy is nurture in particular beliefs, attitudes and values in such a way that children can move securely within the shelter of a particular worldview without that view of life being undermined or challenged too early. Thus Ian MacMullen argues that 'a secure grounding in a coherent primary culture teaches children the nature and value of personal commitment and wards off the kind of listlessness that can inhibit autonomy just as much as lack of critical reflection'.[31]

The importance of having a secure grounding notwithstanding, there is a place for reason and the development of understanding and judgement in every class in the primary school. This is because the dialogue between faith and reason is integral to Catholic faith at every level. Furthermore, children are now encountering different cultures, religious and non-religious backgrounds (e.g. atheist, secularist, indifferent) from a very young age. Therefore, nurture and initiation into the Catholic religion at primary level must now be done in dialogue with the alternatives in any particular society. In sum, while young children are capable of engaging in critical reflection from the very start, the child's right to a clear religious formation must be delicately balanced with the child's developing capacity for critical thought and their need to understand the cultural and religious differences and the differences of moral viewpoints that they encounter in modern pluralist societies.[32]

Ecumenical and inter-religious learning

It is now recognised that Christian religious education at every level includes ecumenical and inter-religious education which enhances students' capacity to engage with other Christians and with people of other religious traditions and beliefs.[33] The Pontifical Council for Inter-religious Dialogue expressed it well when it stated that 'the Christian who meets other believers is not involved in an activity which is marginal to his or her faith. Rather is it something which arises from the demands of that faith. It flows from faith and should be nourished by faith'.[34]

The Church at the Second Vatican Council adopted a positive, sympathetic, general attitude towards the other religions. It called on Catholics to have a positive attitude to other religions which have to be looked at with true, genuine 'sympathy'. In approaching other religions Catholics will look for the positive aspects of these religions and 'acknowledge ... the spiritual and moral truths' to be found in them.[35] The 2007 document, *Catholic Primary Schools: A Policy for Provision into the Future*, issued by the Irish Catholic Bishops' Conference, states (in section 4:3):

> The Catholic school welcomes diversity and strives for inclusivity: it is open to people of other denominations and other faiths, welcomes them into its community and respects their beliefs .... While it maintains its own ethos and provides religious instruction and formation in the Catholic Faith, the Catholic School sees this diversity as

an opportunity for *dialogue and understanding* with those of different faiths.[36] (emphasis mine.)

Today, children are taught that being Catholic entails having a profound respect for and a willingness to dialogue with people of other religions and worldviews. Children are invited to learn about and from the religions of people in their communities, developing the attitudes and capacities that will enable them both to respect their neighbours and respond to the ethical challenges of living with difference. As was suggested earlier in this text, those who have truly experienced religion in depth may be best placed to respect and understand the religious commitments of others. A deep appreciation of their own religion – Christianity – provides the foundation for genuine empathetic understanding of other religions and worldviews.[37]

Formal ecumenical and inter-religious learning in the Catholic primary school builds on the encounter with difference experienced at home and in the school by inviting children to deepen their awareness and knowledge of difference, to respect the religious traditions and/or beliefs of others, to develop positive attitudes towards people of other religious traditions and beliefs, to learn what religions share in common, to enter into respectful dialogue with others, and to grow in appreciation of their own religious experience, commitment and beliefs in light of the experiences, commitments and beliefs of others.[37]

Conclusion
In Catholic religious education, contemporary theories in the psychological, sociological and educational domains are brought into dialogue with the unique vision of the

person and of personal development that Catholic theology provides. The religious education of young children primarily involves *formation*, in which Christian beliefs, attitudes and practices are learned from an insider's theological point of view. It also includes elements of *critical education* in which children learn to understand and make discerning judgements in relation to their own religion and to critically reflect on Christian faith in relation to other religious and non-religious stances for living. Catholic primary religious education demands an inclusive pedagogy that is faithful to the Catholic tradition while being differentiated, culturally sensitive, and flexible in its presentation. Finally, Catholic primary religious education recognises the need to prepare children for dialogue with other Christians and with people of other religious faiths and stances for living. It is precisely by being securely rooted in a rich Christian spirituality that Catholic children will become persons capable of sharing and appreciating the religious and spiritual insights of people who are different from themselves.

Questions for reflection

» Describe a well-educated Catholic child. Describe a badly educated Catholic child.

» How is legitimate transmission/formation/socialisation/ nurture properly combined with intellectual inquiry, questioning, criticism and openness in the religious education of young children?

» Name two stereotypes of Catholic religious education that you would challenge having read this chapter. How has religious education changed from your parents' time?

Supplementary reading

» G. P. (Joe) Fleming, 'Catholic Church Documents on Religious Education' in M. De Souza et al. (eds), *International Handbook of the Religious, Moral and Spiritual Dimensions in Education*, (Dordrecht: Springer, 2006), 607–20.

» Congregation for Catholic Education, *Educating to Intercultural Dialogue in Catholic Schools: Living in Harmony for a Civilization of Love*, 2013.

» Anne Hession, 'Inter-religious Education and the Future of Religious Education in Catholic Primary Schools', in Gareth Byrne and Patricia Kieran (eds), *Toward Mutual Ground: Pluralism, Religious Education and Diversity in Irish Schools* (Dublin: Columba Press, 2013), 165–73.

» Leonard Franchi and Stephen J. McKinney (Eds), *A Companion to Catholic Education* (Leominster: Gracewing, 2011).

Endnotes

1. Benedict XVI, Encyclical Letter *Deus Caritas Est*, (25 December 2005), 1.
2. Gabriel Moran, 'Whose tolerance?' *Journal of Religious Education* (2006), 54(3): 25.
3. For the need for adaptability in presentation of the faith see John Paul II, *Catechesi Tradendae* (On Catechesis in our time), 1979, paras 38, 49, 53, 59, 92; *Catechism of the Catholic Church* (London: Geoffrey Chapman, 1994), 11; Congregation for the Clergy, *General Directory for Catechesis* (London: Catholic Truth Society, 1997), 119–20, 132, 156, 141–2, 246, 249, 279.
4. Kieran Scott, 'Three Traditions of Religious Education' in Jeff Astley and Leslie J. Francis, *Critical Perspectives on Christian Education* (Leominster, Herefordshire: Fowler Wright Books, 1988), 285.
5. Despite recent teachings from the Holy See which see catechesis and religious education as distinct but complementary fields, the Magisterium of the Catholic Church has yet to offer a document which offers a rationale for the conceptual framework, aims, purposes and methodologies of *school-based* religious education. In the absence of such a document, contemporary religious educators tend to draw on principles of catechesis, contemporary theological resources, as well as on the psychological and social sciences for the formation of Catholic educational theories. See John L. Elias, 'Whatever Happened to Catholic Philosophy of Education', *Religious Education* (1999), 94(1): 92–110; Leonard Franchi, 'Catechesis and Religious Education: a Case Study From Scotland', *Religious Education* (2013), 108(5): 467–81.
6. Peter R. Hobson and John S. Edwards, *Religious Education in a Pluralist Society: the key philosophical issues* (London: Routledge Falmer: Woburn Press, 1999), 22.
7. Jeff Astley, *The Philosophy of Christian Religious Education* (Birmingham, Ala.: Religious Education Press, 1994), 122.
8. Gabriel Moran, 'The Aims of Religious Education' in Maria Harris and Gabriel Moran, *Reshaping Religious Education: Conversations on Contemporary Practice* (Louisville, Kentucky: Westminster/ John Knox Press, 1998), 30, 39–41.
9. Astley's description of formative education and critical education is found in Astley, ibid., 78. On the importance of educational language, see Thomas H. Groome, *Christian Religious Education* (San Francisco: Harper & Row, 1980), 23–7; Gabriel Moran, 'Religious Education after Vatican II', in David Efroymson and John Raines (eds), *Open Catholicism: The Tradition at its Best* (Collegeville, Minn: Liturgical Press, 1997), 156–7; and Astley, ibid., 24–9.
10. Edwin Cox, 'Understanding Religion and Religious Understanding', *British Journal of Religious Education* (1983), 6(1): 3–7. John Sullivan argues that critical solidarity with a religious tradition fosters a sense of belonging, commitment and distinctiveness in *Catholic Education: Distinctive and Inclusive* (Dordrecht: Kluwer Academic Publishers, 2001), 35.
11. The Second Vatican Council (often called 'Vatican II') was the last great Ecumenical Council of the Catholic Church which addressed relations between the Catholic Church and the modern world. It lasted from 1962 to 1965. For a fuller overview of the understanding of Revelation proposed at Vatican II, see Dermot A. Lane, *The Experience of God*. (Dublin: Veritas, 2003), 66–71.

12. Kate Siejk, 'Toward a Holistic Religious Education: Reflections and Pedagogical Possibilities', *Religious Education* (1994), 89(2): 273. See also Parker J. Palmer, *The Courage to Teach: Exploring the Inner Landscape of a Teacher's Life* (San Francisco: Jossey-Bass Publishers, 1998), Chapter 4, for an excellent critique of what he terms 'the objectivist myth' of knowing.

13. Dermot A. Lane, 'Foreword' in Gareth Byrne and Patricia Kieran (eds), *Toward Mutual Ground: Pluralism, Religious Education and Diversity in Irish Schools* (Dublin: Columba Press, 2013), 20. On transcendence in human knowing, see Palmer, ibid., 105ff.

14. Palmer, ibid., 56.

15. Thomas H. Groome outlines the three dimensions of knowing in Christian faith in *Christian Religious Education: Sharing our Story and Vision* (San Francisco: Harper&Row, 1980), 56–63.

16. Given the distinctive epistemology that underpins the Catholic approach to religious education, it is not surprising to find words like 'imagine', 'respond', 'discern', 'depict', 'evoke', 'wonder', 'meditate', 'explore' alongside words like 'analyse', 'evaluate' and 'explain' in the language of the Catholic religious education curriculum.

17. Jack G. Priestly, 'Towards Finding the Hidden Curriculum: a Consideration of the Spiritual Dimension of Experience in Curriculum Planning', *British Journal of Religious Education* (1985), 7(3): 116. On the distinctiveness of Christian epistemology, see Debra Dean Murphy, *Teaching that Transforms: Worship as the Heart of Christian Education*, (Grand Rapids, Michigan: Brazos Press, 2004), Chapter 4.

18. Andrew G. McGrady, 'A Metaphor and Model Paradigm of Religious Thinking', *British Journal of Religious Education* (1987)9: 2, 92.

19. Edwin Cox, 'Understanding Religion and Religious Understanding', *British Journal of Religious Education* (1983) 6, part 1.

20. Gabriel Moran, 'Two Languages of Religious Education' in J. Astley & L. J. Francis (eds), ibid., 45.

21. See Vatican II, *Dignitatis Humanae* (Declaration on Religious Freedom), 1965.

22. Sullivan, ibid., 35.

23. John Sullivan, 'Faith Schools: a culture within a culture in a changing world' in M. de Souza et al. (eds.), *International Handbook of the Religious, Moral and Spiritual Dimensions in Education* (Dordrecht: Springer, 2006), 940.

24. Luigi Giussani, *The Risk of Education: Discovering our Ultimate Destiny* (New York: Crossroad Publishing, 2001). The Jesuit theologian and philosopher, Bernard Lonergan, suggested four key virtues – attentiveness, intelligence, reasonableness and responsibility – for the kind of appropriation and critical decision suggested here.

25. See Astley's arguments for a 'qualified critical approach' to religious education in Astley, ibid., 83 and 94–9. For a helpful critique of the 'objectivist' theory of knowing that dominates in education today, see the work of Parker J. Palmer. Palmer offers the image of 'trothfulness' – a commitment to living out the truths that one knows, as an alternative to the dominant paradigm. Parker J. Palmer, *To Know as we are Known: Education as a Spiritual Journey* (New York: HarperSanFrancisco, 1993), Chapters 1, 2 and 4.

26. See Vatican II, *Declaration on Religious Liberty* (1965), a. 2 and 9. Congregation for Catholic Education, *The Religious Dimension of Education in a Catholic School*, 1988, 6.

27. Dermot A. Lane, 'Catholic Education and the Primary School in the Twenty-First Century', in Eugene Duffy (ed.), *Catholic Primary Education: Facing New Challenges* (Dublin: The Columba Press, 2012) 43.

28. John Hull, *Studies in Religion and Education* (Lewes, Sussex: Falmer Press, 1984), 220.

29. Congregation for Catholic Education, *The Religious Dimension of Education in a Catholic School* (1988), para. 6. See also Congregation for Catholic Education, *Lay Catholics in Schools: Witnesses to Faith*, 1982, no. 42.

30. Astley, ibid., 274.

31. Ian MacMullen, 'Education for Autonomy: the Role of Religious Elementary Schools', in *Journal of Philosophy of Education* (2004), 38(4), 605.

32. On this subject, see Elmer John Thiessen, who advocates a 'two-phase approach' – first 'the initiation or nurture phase', then 'a gradual opening-up phase' where the children 'are exposed to other influences, other beliefs, though still from the vantage point of the tradition into which they were first initiated'. Elmer J. Thiessen, *Teaching for Commitment: Liberal Education, Indoctrination, and Christian Nurture* (London: McGill-Queen's University Press, 1993), 225–42. For an opposing view, see Karl Ernst Nipkow, 'Christian education and the charge of indoctrination', in Dennis Bates, Gloria Durka and Friedrich Schweitzer (eds), *Education, Religion and Society* (London, New York: Routledge, 2006), 108–9.

33. See Congregation for Catholic Education, *Educating to Intercultural Dialogue in Catholic Schools*, 2013.

34. Pontifical Council for Inter-religious Dialogue, 'Letter to Presidents of Bishops' Conferences on the Spirituality of Dialogue', Vatican City, 3 March, 1999, 1. Available on the Vatican website, http://www.vatican.va.

35. *Decree on the Relation of the Church to non-Christian Religions (Nostra Aetate)*, no. 2. See also *Lumen Gentium*, n.16; Ad Gentes, nos. 9, 11.

36. Irish Catholic Bishops' Conference, *Catholic Primary Schools: A Policy for Provision into the Future*, (Dublin: Veritas, 2007), 5.

37. See Anne Hession, 'Inter-religious Education and the Future of Religious Education in Catholic Primary Schools', in Gareth Byrne and Patricia Kieran (eds), ibid., 165–76.

CHAPTER SIX
THE CATHOLIC PRIMARY RELIGIOUS EDUCATION CURRICULUM FOR IRELAND

In the context of Catholic education, no awareness of distinctiveness is possible without awareness of difference, and no possibility of inclusiveness remains without there being a distinct body (of people and truth) to which one can belong and by which one can be included.[1]

JOHN SULLIVAN

There is no direct connection between belief in the exclusive truth of one's own commitments and intolerance of those who hold contrary commitments. Belief in the superiority of humanism over Christianity, for example, does not (logically) sanction humanists to be intolerant of Christians. Superiority of belief need not issue in an attitude of superiority! The two are quite distinct.[2]

L. PHILIP BARNES

THE RELIGIOUS DIMENSION OF EDUCATION IN A CATHOLIC SCHOOL includes the formal religious education curriculum, the liturgical, sacramental and prayer life of the school, as well as opportunities for students to engage in activities that build Christian community and reach out to those in need. Ideally, for baptised children, the formal religious education *curriculum* (sometimes called 'curriculum religion') is supported and completed by catechesis, liturgical celebration and social justice activities in the home and in the parish. This chapter offers some reflections on the formal religious education curriculum for Irish Catholic primary schools.

What are we doing? A theological perspective

Christian faith in its essence is a gift of God. Faith may be understood in two ways: as a process of developing personal belief and trust in God and as a specific content which is believed (the Catholic faith, a body of knowledge). But far from being an isolated act of the individual, faith is essentially shared. God approaches me and calls me to Godself, *together with* every other person created by God. Personal faith is sustained by the believing community, and every Christian has a responsibility to share his or her faith with others and hand on the gift he or she has received. Each of these aspects of faith is integral to Catholic religious education.

Catholic faith is first and foremost about developing a relationship with God the Father, through Jesus Christ, in the Holy Spirit. The Catholic religious education curriculum serves the goal of inviting students to understand what it means to become a disciple of Jesus. Learning how to be a *Christian* is learning how to encounter, know and follow Jesus and to place your trust in the activity and presence of God within all of human life. Catholic religious education invites children into a particular kind of personal transformation which can be termed 'conversion' or 'holiness'. Holiness for a Christian is living in relationship with Jesus Christ in such a way that the person is rooted in love. Accepting the presence of God's Holy Spirit in each and every circumstance of life, such a person lives a life of justice and compassion, serving others and making a difference in society and the world.

This is the *raison d'être* of the Catholic religious education curriculum from a theological perspective.[3] Now we will examine what this understanding of 'being a Christian' or 'becoming holy' means in *educational* terms.

What are we doing? An educational perspective

The aim of the Irish Catholic Pre-school and Primary religious education curriculum is:

> To help children mature in relation to their spiritual, moral and religious lives, through their encounter with, exploration and celebration of the Catholic faith.

This aim conveys the understanding that Catholic religious education is an academic discipline which invites people to acquire the knowledge (the content of the Catholic Faith), forms of knowing, attitudes, emotions, values, skills, moral actions and sensibilities that being Christian involves. This aim gives the curriculum a clear educational focus by saying what exactly religious education in the Catholic school contributes to the personal development of the child. Furthermore, this aim applies the notion of differentiation to the task of religious education in the recognition that all pupils in Catholic schools can be helped to mature in relation to their spiritual, moral and religious lives, through responding to and exploring the Catholic religious tradition, rather than conforming to it unthinkingly or with an assumed level of prior commitment.[4]

Helping children mature in relation to their spiritual, moral and religious lives means helping them to learn specific skills of Christian spiritual, moral and religious literacy, such as:

» understanding beliefs and doctrines about God, Jesus, the Church and its mission, the origins and purpose of human life, human nature and the world;
» learning how to come to 'know' in Christian faith (metaphorical thinking, prayer, wonder, imagination, reasoning);
» developing the capacity for critical Christian reflection and theological thinking;
» learning how to participate in the prayer and worship of the Church;
» learning Christian moral actions, personal and social responsibility and ways of moral reasoning;
» developing Christian emotions and feelings;
» learning the attitudes and dispositions of Christian spirituality and the Christian virtues;
» learning about other Christian traditions and other religious traditions.

Christian faith is *encountered* because faith has a content which has been revealed by God. Believers do not just come up with beliefs themselves; what is to be believed is proposed to them by God. God is revealed in experience and history, in the whole of creation and in particular in the life, death and resurrection of Jesus Christ. People are invited to respond to this in faith. This is why Catholic religious education has an abiding commitment to 'handing on' a body of religious language, religious doctrines, religious practices and religious truths. This cumulative wisdom of the past is generally referred to as 'tradition'.[5] The core of this tradition is the offer of an encounter with the person of Jesus Christ and his 'good news of salvation'. This encounter with Jesus is mediated now through Sacred Scripture, teachings and practices that have been handed down through the ages as the Church has continued to live and reflect on the Christian faith. The Catholic tradition includes interpretations of Sacred Scripture, articles of faith, doctrines, official creedal statements of the Church, the Lord's Prayer, the commandments, ethical principles, rituals, symbols, spiritualities, theologies, lives of the saints, music, art, architecture and so on.

Christian faith is *explored* because every child is invited to respond to the living presence of God in his or her own life. As faith is a free and personal act, this response must be a free response that engages the child's critical and creative faculties. By engaging with the sacred texts, doctrines and beliefs of the Church community, children are enabled to respond to the revelation and presence of God reflected in Scripture and tradition, in creation and in their own lives. Christians believe the risen Christ is still with the people of God as they seek to encounter and recognise God's presence and will for their lives in the world today. Therefore, religious education often involves relating the lived experience of children with Scripture and the Church's tradition in such a way that they begin to discern what the 'good news of salvation' means for their own lives. Lessons often start with the learners' experience and lead them to reflect upon it in the light of the Gospel. This method is called alternatively *correlation* or *praxis*. The goal is to set up a profound relationship between life and faith, between theory and practice, between faith and reason, between human experience and Christian faith, with the intended outcome of lived Christian faith.

Finally, Christian faith is *celebrated* because God is here, in the midst of our lives and communities; God's reign has begun in Jesus and our first response is joy and thanksgiving. When we realise that our lives are gift, we know that we do not have to earn God's love and compassion. We simply accept the gift and give thanks. The religious education of young children is focused primarily on this gift. The opportunity to experience God's love and to celebrate it is an important prerequisite for an autonomous and genuine response of the child to that love. As Sofia Cavalletti has warned, to move too quickly to the child's response teaches them that God's love is something to be earned, that religious living is a burden and that being religious is about measuring one's righteousness before God.[6]

Religious literacy
What does it mean for a child to be religiously literate in the Catholic faith? The curriculum defines 'religious literacy' as:

> The ability to understand and use, in the young child's day-to-day life, a repertoire of practices and/or 'ways of knowing' related to the Christian religion using reading, writing, listening, speaking, viewing, drawing,

music, movement, critical and creative thinking, and multimedia texts of traditional and new information and communications technologies.[7]

There are a number of different dimensions to being religiously literate in the Catholic tradition.[8] First, it involves *understanding* the given content of the Catholic faith. Central concepts include the transcendence and immanence of God, the humanity and divinity of Jesus the Christ and his unique role in the salvation of all, together with the understanding that the Church, as the community of disciples of Jesus, is the sacrament of God's salvation in the world today. The kind of understanding aimed at here is not about passive reception and rote learning of a list of revealed truths. Children learn how to listen, learn from and respond to what has been revealed by God and they are invited to judge and decide what this might mean for their lives. (For more on the kind of knowing promoted here, see Chapter Five). Higher-order thinking skills such as explaining, problem-solving, predicting, analysing, questioning, evaluating and justifying are important for religious thinking; so too is use of the imagination, creative process and metaphorical thinking – capacities which are integral to the process of understanding in religion. Furthermore, a child who understands Christian faith will know that there is an important affective dimension to religious belief. A crucial distinction here is that between 'believing *that*' something is so (e.g. that God exists, that Jesus is God, that persons are created by God, etc.) and 'believing *in*' God or Jesus, in the sense of placing one's faith and complete trust in God.[9] A religiously literate child is one who is beginning to know the difference!

Secondly, religious literacy also involves being able *to communicate* in and about one's religion. To communicate is first and foremost to encounter other people. As Stefan Altmeyer explains, 'Christian faith is concentrated on the idea that the way of experiencing God involves an encounter with the self and with others (including people of other religions). This is why sensitising to personal relations must be at the heart of religious learning'.[10] The first step in being able to communicate in my own religion involves developing a specific spiritual, moral and religious vocabulary. Given that many children are immersed in a largely secular environment before coming to school, religious words such as 'altar', 'genuflect', 'disciple' and 'fasting' may be learned in school for the first time. Furthermore, learning to communicate in the Christian religion involves learning how to appreciate and respond to sacred texts, stories, music and poetry. It includes learning how to pray, how to communicate in liturgy, and how to respond artistically to religious experience. Communication skills include talking and writing with understanding and insight about spiritual, moral and religious ideas, reflecting critically and creatively on spiritual, moral and religious issues, and debating and using reasoned arguments. The ability to communicate *in*, *through* and *about* one's own religion has increased importance in our time, as Christians are called to dialogue with people of differing religions and cultures.

Thirdly, to be religiously literate in Christian faith involves *participating*. There is something about coming to know in Christian faith that is intimately tied to practice. As Danièle Hervieu-Léger points out, 'the process of believing (as compared with any specific belief) includes not only particular convictions, but also the practices, languages, gestures and habits in which these beliefs are inscribed. Such believing is belief in action, belief lived out'.[11] When children are invited to participate in experiences of prayer, silence and meditation it develops their capacity for personal prayer and for participation in the Church's liturgy. When they get involved in practical activities associated with Christian charity, stewardship of creation and social justice, they grow in moral awareness and authentic Christian concern for the poor, for human equality and the integrity of creation. When they are encouraged to work with others in research projects, drama activities and common educational tasks it helps them develop responsibility, interdependence and commitment.

Fourthly, being religiously literate in Christian faith means developing a distinctly *Christian* spirituality. Pope John Paul II described Christian spirituality as follows:

Spirituality is 'life in Christ' and 'in the Spirit', which is accepted in faith, expressed in love and inspired by hope, and so becomes the daily life of the Church community. In this sense, by spirituality, which is the goal of conversion, we mean 'not a part of life, but the whole of life guided by the Holy Spirit'. Among the many elements of spirituality which all Christians must make their own, prayer holds a pre-eminent place. Prayer leads Christians 'little by little to acquire a contemplative view of reality, enabling them to recognize God in every moment and in everything; to contemplate God in every person; to seek his will in all that happens'.... Christian spirituality is nourished above all by a constant sacramental life, since the Sacraments are the root and endless source of God's grace which believers need to sustain them on their earthly pilgrimage .... It should also be noted that this spirituality is not opposed to the social responsibilities of the Christian life. On the contrary, in following the path of prayer, believers become more conscious of the Gospel's demands and of their duties towards others.[12]

Christian spirituality is following Jesus in the practice of the love of God and neighbour. It is rooted in the experience of a personal encounter with Jesus Christ, the implications of which are lived out in community with others. In the Catholic school, children are taught how to live their lives in the Spirit of Jesus as they encounter him in prayer, in the Word of God, in the sacraments and in their own lives. They are enabled to understand how a Christian spirituality is sustained in the community of faith, the Church. The ultimate goal is to teach children how to develop their relationship with God through prayer, so that they are drawn into the very life of God as Father, Son and Holy Spirit (Trinity). Education to and for prayer is at the heart of the spiritual education curriculum in the Catholic school. Through the experience of prayer the child is invited to understand that the act of faith in God is deeply personal as well as social and that they have a spiritual life that is intimately connected to their unique individuality.

As Irish society becomes increasingly secular, education in a Christian spirituality becomes a counter-cultural activity. In this context, one of the first tasks of the religious educator is to create the environment in which pupils recognise the spiritual dimension of their own being. This involves developing the basic awareness that to be human is to be spiritual and that spiritual experience is ordinary human experience – a dimension of their lives that exists precisely *in* their lives as children and not as a domain set apart from those actual lives. In other words, being spiritual has something to do with becoming attuned to the presence of God in their everyday experiences of working, suffering, love, joy, wonder, compassion and their thirst for justice. In this context also, it is important that children are helped to explore the challenges to Christian spirituality posed by the other frameworks of meaning found in Irish culture. For example, they might be invited to explore and critically reflect on films, stories, advertisements, slogans, and the lyrics of songs for the messages they contain about self, others, life, death and meaning. These can then be compared to the message and values of Jesus Christ.

A spiritually literate child will be able to reflect critically and creatively on what are called 'ultimate questions', viz. questions about life, death, aloneness, freedom, identity, belonging, love, interdependence and the afterlife. Catholic religious educators will offer children the resources of the Christian faith tradition as they explore those questions. Children will be helped to understand that, for Christians, each of these questions and experiences is given an additional meaning because of the life, death and resurrection of Jesus Christ. In other words, these experiences are interpreted and lived differently in light of Christian faith.

Fifthly, a religiously literate child is one who has the capacity to dialogue with people of other cultures and religions. Openness towards and readiness for dialogue with adherents of other religions is an integral part of being Christian. Skills of inter-religious literacy enable children to be able to speak the public language of religion, to comprehend and appreciate the place of religious and philosophical beliefs and practices in human life, to understand the need for dialogue among Christians, to develop powers of empathy for and sensitivity towards people of other religions and cultures, to explore the beliefs and practices of other world religions, to enter into dialogue with people of other religions and beliefs and to foster awareness of shared values such as justice, peace, solidarity, tolerance and freedom.[13]

The four strands

The content of the curriculum is divided into four interrelated strands: Christian Faith, The Word of God, Liturgy/Prayer and Christian Morality. Together these four strands outline the knowledge and understanding, skills and processes that make up the learning to be achieved at each level of the curriculum. The strands should not be understood as discrete areas of learning, as they overlap and interact to form a holistic learning experience for the child.[14]

Christian faith

Teaching and learning in this strand enables children to learn the key truths, doctrines and practices of the Catholic religious tradition. The proclamation of the Christian message (*Kerygma*) – the announcement of the Good News of Jesus Christ – is found at the core of the Christian Faith strand. Throughout the curriculum, children are introduced to God's loving plan of salvation revealed to us in Jesus Christ and brought to fruition through his Church. Most importantly, children are invited to a deeper understanding and appreciation of what it means to be a disciple of Jesus, and of how to participate in the life and mission of the Church. They are also taught about the witness to that mission given by the saints and by holy members of the people of God.

The Word of God

The Word of God strand introduces children in an age-appropriate way to Sacred Scripture in the life of the Church. Sacred Scripture is the story of God's past blessings on the people of God, as well as an inspired Word for the present to enable the Church community to recognise God's presence among us. Christian religious education is rooted in the central stories of Scripture and, in particular, the story of Jesus Christ. By listening to and understanding Sacred Scripture, children come to know the person of Jesus Christ and begin to relate to him and to his salvific mission. They learn from the Bible what it means to be a disciple of Jesus in the community of faith. An awareness of the history of salvation enables children to become more aware of God's ongoing salvific action in the life of his people.

The Word of God strand introduces children to God's loving plan of salvation in Scripture. As children discover biblical events in the three great 'moments' of salvation history (creation, salvation, parousia[15]), they are invited to recognise God's presence in their own lives and experiences. The word of God is interpreted in the Catholic community under the guidance of the Holy Spirit. Children in Catholic primary schools grow in their familiarity with the Bible and develop the ability to authentically interpret the Sacred Scriptures in light of Church teaching, applying them in relevant and fruitful ways to the circumstances of their lives as children.

Liturgy/prayer

The Bible tells the story of salvation. The liturgy celebrates and makes it present. So, through liturgy, a person can have an *experience* of divine presence and concern. In fact, the liturgy is the primary way in which Christians celebrate and give thanks for the redeeming presence of God in their midst. Teaching and learning in the Liturgy/Prayer strand enables children to engage with liturgical signs, symbols and rituals which nurture their relationship with God as Father, Son and Spirit, and to develop their capacity for personal prayer and for participation in the liturgy of the Church.

Liturgy involves learning by doing. Through participation in classroom rituals, children learn the Christian language of ritual – praise, thanks, confession and mourning.[16] These languages enable children to worship God and to express the deepest desires and movements of the human heart. In addition, individual ritual actions (such as lighting a candle before a statue or meditating in stillness) and communal ritual actions (such as making the sign of the cross or the sign of peace) offer children a whole-bodied way of articulating the mystery of God.

Children also learn the language of religious ritual as they participate in the liturgies celebrated in the local church, the most important of which is the Sunday Eucharist. The readings, prayers, gestures and symbols of the Eucharist work together over long periods of time to shape children's attitudes, understandings and faith commitments. Ideally education in religious narratives, symbols and rituals in the primary school classroom should allow children to practise the patterns of language and behaviour they are acquiring through their experience in the local Christian faith community.

Christian morality
Teaching and learning in the Christian Morality strand enables children to grow in awareness of their identity

as persons created in the image and likeness of God and called to live in loving, respectful relationship with God, other human persons and the whole of creation. They are introduced to Jesus as the model for living an ethical life and to the moral teachings of the Church that teach them how to live as his disciples. Children are formed in gospel values and in love of God and neighbour and they learn that the goal of Christian moral life is only reached by the aid of the grace of the Holy Spirit. Children also learn the importance of prayer, asceticism and the sacraments in nurturing their moral lives. They learn to cultivate an upright and informed conscience and develop their ability for moral reasoning as they confront moral dilemmas.

Skills (outcomes)

Each of the four strands contain broad outcomes or skills which outline what children are invited to know and understand, and how they will interact with the knowledge and concepts outlined in the strand. The articulation of the curriculum in terms of educational outcomes offers teachers a clear focus for their work. It also facilitates the assessment and evaluation of students' learning outcomes in a way that is helpful for future planning. The outcomes allow teachers to see at a glance how the learning develops from level to level throughout the school. This sequencing across levels also assists teachers in planning learning activities to cater for diverse student abilities. The outcomes are outlined in a spiral way so that the core outcomes (of which there are 25 in total) return at every level. An example of how this works in practice is illustrated in Table 5:

Table 5: An Illustration of the Spiral Curriculum: sample *objectives* that correspond to each outcome *at each level* are provided

Strand	Core Outcome/ Skill	Sample Objective Level 1	Sample Objective Level 2	Sample Objective Level 3	Sample Objective Level 4
Christian Faith	Discuss Christian beliefs using a range of religious words.	Identify that Jesus was born on Christmas day.	Name Jesus as the Good Shepherd.	Discuss ways of being a Christian community.	Identify the three persons of the Trinity and how the Trinity is honoured.
Word of God	Describe the behaviour, intentions and feelings of characters in Sacred Scripture texts.	Describe how Jesus might have felt when he got lost in the temple.	Discuss why Jesus forgave Zacchaeus.	Tell the Easter story from the perspective of Mary Magdalene or Peter.	Present the story of Jesus and the woman at the well with the woman as narrator.
Liturgy and Prayer	Explore symbols, feelings, words, gestures and actions in prayer, liturgy and sacraments.	Make an Advent wreath with the teacher.	Make an Advent calendar.	Make a book illustrating in words and pictures the order of events at baptism.	Explore liturgical objects used in the celebration of Confirmation.
Christian Morality	Show respect towards self and others.	Explore my senses as gifts from God.	Discuss how we can live like Jesus.	Discuss the uniqueness of each person, created by God.	Make practical moral application of the Sermon on the Mount.
No. of Outcomes		25	25 + 22 = **47**	**47**+ 19 = **66**	**66**+21 = **87**

Faith formation goals

The development of lived Christian faith in discipleship of Jesus is the ultimate horizon within which religious education is carried out in Irish primary Catholic schools. While religious education is open to all students enrolled in such schools, nevertheless, it is expected that many children in Catholic pre-schools and primary schools will be baptised Catholics, and good religious education will aim to help them to grow towards maturity in Christian faith. Teachers will always be conscious of the need to support the on-going faith development and catechesis of these children when planning lessons. Faith formation goals are provided in the curriculum to guide teachers in this important work.

The primary focus of faith formation goals in the primary school is on fostering an encounter with the person of Jesus and on enabling the experience of intimacy and communion with him (worship). Children are invited to learn from Jesus' actions, his teaching, the teaching of his Church, and to think and judge like him, in the religious education curriculum (knowledge of the content of the Faith). Finally, it is hoped that children will develop a commitment to participate in the mission and ministry of Jesus, our Saviour, living their Christian faith, in the Church community, for the Kingdom of God (ethical living as Jesus' disciples).

The relationship between teaching and faith development is different from the way teaching relates to knowledge and skill development in religious education. This is because of the complexity of spiritual development and of the complex ways in which it may or may not be related to classroom teaching/learning processes. Ultimately, teachers need educational goals that translate into educational practices that have a clear sequence of progression and that are assessable. These goals have been distinguished from faith formation goals in the curriculum so that teaching does not become vague and haphazard. Unlike the religious education outcomes in the curriculum, teachers' hopes or goals in the area of faith development will not be assessed, as it is inappropriate to formally assess personal or spiritual change in students.

Conclusion

The Catholic Primary School Religious Education Curriculum is the first religious education curriculum written for Catholic primary schools in Ireland. The curriculum is innovative in that it empowers teachers to take into account the diverse levels of familiarity with and commitment to the Catholic tradition prevalent among pupils. The curriculum is inclusive in that it is open to all children whose parents wish them to learn *about*, *from* or *into* the Christian religious tradition. The curriculum articulates clearly what is meant by religious literacy in the Catholic tradition and distinguishes educational outcomes from faith formation outcomes in a way that honours the nature of Christian faith and the discipline of education. Finally, the curriculum supports Catholic children's development of a distinctive religious identity while being respectful of diversity and open to learning from the religious and non-religious worldviews of others.

Questions for reflection

» Discuss the concept of 'Revelation'. What does it mean to be an adherent of a revealed religion?

» Using the categories of understanding, communicating, participating, spiritual literacy and inter-religious literacy, examine your own level of religious literacy. If you are a Catholic, where are your weaknesses and strengths? If you are committed to another religious tradition, are there aspects you would share with Catholics? What other aspects of religious literacy are important in your religious tradition?

» What aspects of religious literacy should be emphasised in the public school setting? Which aspects should be emphasised in the home and in the parish?

» Compare your understanding of Christian spirituality with other spiritual frameworks offered by Irish primary schools.

Supplementary reading

» Irish Episcopal Conference, *Catholic Preschool and Primary School Religious Education Curriculum for Ireland* (Dublin: Veritas, 2015).

» John Sullivan, *Learning the language of Faith* (Essex: Matthew James Publishing Ltd., 2010).

Endnotes

1. John Sullivan, *Catholic Education: Distinctive and Inclusive* (Dordrecht: Kluwer, 2001), 29.

2. L. Philip Barnes, 'Religious Education and the Misrepresentation of Religion', in Marius Felderhof, Penny Thompson and David Torevell (eds), *Inspiring Faith in Schools* (Hampshire: Ashgate, 2007), 84.

3. For a more detailed exploration of the theological rationale for Christian religious education, see Anne Hession and Patricia Kieran, 'Christian Religious Education: Purpose and Process', in *Children, Catholicism and Religious Education*, (Dublin: Veritas, 2005), 154–8.

4. For reflections on the relevance of differentiation applied to the religious realm within Catholic schools and the educational implications of appropriating the living tradition of Catholicism, see Sullivan, ibid., Chapters 6 and 7.

5. On the concept of 'Tradition', see Brendan Leahy, 'Tradition' in Anne Hession and Patricia Kieran (eds), *Exploring Theology: Making Sense of the*

Catholic Tradition (Dublin: Veritas, 2007), 90–100. On the Catholic Church's understanding of 'living tradition', see Sullivan, ibid., Chapter 7.

6. On the enjoyment of God as the basis of the Christian moral life, see Sofia Cavelletti, *The Religious Potential of the Child* (New York: Paulist Press, 1983), 151–55 and Sofia Cavelletti, *The Religious Potential of the Child 6–12 years old* (Chicago: Liturgy Training Publications, 2002), 84–96,

7. Irish Episcopal Conference, *Catholic Preschool and Primary Religious Education Curriculum for Ireland*, (Dublin: Veritas, 2015). On the importance of interpreting the skill paradigm according to a humanistic vision and on the need to eschew a merely functional view of education which reduces education to skills about knowing and knowing how to do, see Congregation for Catholic Education, 'Educating Today and Tomorrow; a renewing passion', Instrumentum Laboris, 2014, 12.

8. There may be supernatural changes in a person that lie beneath the skills of spiritual, moral and religious literacy outlined in the curriculum, changes which cannot be known by observation and which derive from the grace of God. The curriculum does not deny that faith is ultimately a gift of God. However, Catholic religious education needs a definition of being a Christian that is of practical use to teachers.

9. Martin Buber, *Two Types of Faith* (New York: HarperCollins, 1951).

10. Stefan Altmeyer, 'Competences in Inter-religious Learning', in K. Engebretson et al. (eds), *International Handbook of Inter-religious Education* (Dordrecht: Springer, 2010), 634.

11. Danièle Herview-Léger, *La Religion Pour Mémoire* (Paris, Cerf, 1993), 105. I'm indebted to John Sullivan for this citation and translation. See Sullivan, ibid., 10.

12. John Paul II, Post-Synodal Apostolic Exhortation, *Ecclesia in America*, January 22, 1999, no. 29.

13. Congregation for Catholic Education, *Educating to Intercultural Dialogue in Catholic Schools: Living in Harmony for a Civilization of Love*, 2013, nos. 33, 63.

14. For example, the Christian Morality strand could not stand without the Word of God strand as Scripture is a primary source for the moral education of Christians. Similarly, education in the Christian virtues of faith, hope and charity is found in all of the strands.

15. The 'Parousia' is the end of time, when Christ will come again to judge the living and the dead and God will be 'all in all'.

16. Maria Harris and Gabriel Moran, *Reshaping Religious Education: Conversations on Contemporary Practice* (Louisville, Kentucky: Westminster/ John Knox Press, 1998), 34.

CHAPTER SEVEN
CATHOLIC MORAL EDUCATION AT PRIMARY LEVEL

Morality is based on an appreciation of human dignity and its demands — a dignity given a new depth by the Gospel. It concerns the implications for our living and our attitudes which flow from that appreciation.[1]

DONAL MURRAY

I can only answer the question 'What am I to do?' If I can answer the prior question 'of what story or stories do I find myself a part?[2]

ALISTER MACINTYRE

The moral and spiritual aims of Christianity do not centre on producing good citizens or on encouraging reflection on spiritual matters; instead they focus on the need for Christians to emulate the character of Christ and to practise justice and righteousness ... Christian spirituality and morality are concerned with inspiring and encouraging those who trust in Christ for their salvation to obey the moral precepts of the New Testament. It is not that Christians are unspiritual or make poor citizens; it is that Christian spirituality and morality centre on loyalty to God, not on loyalty to the nation state and its evolving legal norms.[3]

L. PHILIP BARNES

MORALITY IS A GUIDE TO WHO WE ARE (OUR CHARACTERS) AND WHAT we do (our conduct). Morality answers the questions, 'What kind of person ought I become and what kind of life ought I live?' When teachers claim to offer children a *moral* or *ethical* education, they are making a claim that they can help children to reach their full potential as human persons in the communities to which they belong. The moral education of young children involves teaching them to hold particular beliefs and to behave in particular ways. At a later stage they will be encouraged to hold those beliefs and practices in a critical perspective as they engage with different ethical points of view. This chapter introduces a few distinctive features of a Catholic approach to moral education at primary level, in the context of alternative ethical approaches. Some common misunderstandings about the Catholic moral education of young children are examined and some distinctive features of the 'Christian morality' strand of the Catholic Primary Religious Education Curriculum are outlined.

The distinctiveness of Catholic moral education

The Catholic approach to moral education invites children to understand that reaching their potential for goodness and for living a good human life includes responding to and nourishing their capacity for relationship with *God*. For Christians, God is the criterion of meaning for a good human life and it is God who invites us to live in community in ways which are life-giving for all persons. In this sense, Christian morality involves learning how to respond to something *beyond the self* as a basis for one's moral life. As philosopher Charles Taylor has explained, religions often ask us to consider a perspective on human life where the aim or goal cannot be entirely explained in terms of the search for a fuller, better, richer, more satisfying human life. Christianity draws our attention to a moral vision that asks us to see a point beyond the search for a full life (although this is a worthy goal) to something or someone that can command our fullest *love*, a way of life that has meaning even in the midst of suffering and death.[4]

For Christians, furthermore, to act morally towards other people is to accept that *God* invites and calls us to serve others and to respect their dignity and independence.[5] As Rowan Williams explains, being moral for Christians 'has more to do with seeing the other person as loved by God rather than acknowledging them only as another human being.'[6] To live morally out of a faith perspective, explains Williams, is to experience and understand myself as:

> invited to make myself answerable for the good, the human welfare and spiritual health, of the human other … in part because of how I have learned to 'read' the world around, reading it as suggesting that an agency independent of any circumstance within the world has 'taken responsibility' for *my* welfare — has not only given life in general, but put at my disposal the life that is its own.[7]

A corollary of this perspective is that Christians understand their ethical actions as part of the creative and compassionate action of God's presence and action in the world. Christian moral living involves imitating a master – Jesus Christ – who not only shows us how to love but whose spirit *empowers* us to continue living a life of love even when to do so is difficult and even counter-cultural. For a

Christian then, *love* is what inspires a good moral life and *love* is the energy that empowers good and ethical actions in the world. Because God has made Godself known to us in Jesus; because this God has created us with a divine identity and a divine destiny, Christians never understand morality as obeying rules and regulations, but as the struggle to identify and move with the direction of God's creative and compassionate action in the world.[8]

Another important difference between Catholic morality and secular moralities is that Catholic morality is taught within the context of a *longer-term* perspective on the future of humanity, history and creation. For Christians, life is lived in the light of eternity: present actions and concerns are interpreted in light of our ultimate destination with God in heaven. As Curtis Hancock explains:

> A Christian believes ... that human freedom burdens human beings with moral judgement; and that human beings will eventually answer to God for the moral quality of their conduct. ... According to Christianity, human beings by our choices and actions work out the social and historical meaning of our lives, a social experience and history that can be fully measured only by the judgement of God at the end of time.[9]

In the Catholic school, children are offered a hope-filled interpretation of human life and death in light of the life, death and resurrection of Jesus as the Christ. The salvation offered by Christ promises a future in which there will be a New Heaven and a New Earth, when Christ comes again at the end of time. In this context moral education includes teaching children that their lives have a 'temporal and eternal significance',[10] that one day good will triumph over evil, that the suffering of all those who suffer in the cause of justice and all the victims of history will not be forgotten by God, and that every act of love and justice on behalf of humanity and the well-being of the earth will endure unto eternal life. The possibilities for hope, fulfilment and transformation within our human experience, offered by Jesus Christ, stimulates our shared responsibility for bringing about a more just and fair world in this life before His Second Coming at the end of time.[11]

Some misunderstandings about Catholic moral education

There is no doubt that many Irish Catholics have been badly served in the domain of moral education in the past. A too-early emphasis on personal sin, understood as a transgression of God's law, before people experienced the love and overwhelming mercy of God, prevented many people of earlier generations from developing a healthy Christian spirituality. As a result many misunderstandings of the purposes and processes of Catholic moral education abound in popular consciousness that need to be examined and critiqued. The first misconception is that Catholic moral education of young children is about forcing conformity to a set of moral rules and regulations. This is to misunderstand the place of moral principles and norms in a healthy Christian morality. It is important to stress that Catholic moral educators are concerned with the development of character and virtues rather than enforcing obedience to moral rules. Moral development is about being invited to *be* a certain kind of person, and to live in a certain type of community in response to the loving invitation of God.

A second misunderstanding is that Catholic morality entails making children feel guilty, sinful and bad. This is a fundamental error for it suggests that Catholics are morally good in response to fear! Again this idea is understandable because of many Catholics' experience of authoritarian forms of moral teaching in the past. However, for Catholics, *experiencing* the love of God and of one's identity as a child of God, and not fear, is the only basis for living morally. This is such an important point that it bears repeating: as long as people are prevented from discovering their unity with God, the divine presence at the heart of their being, then Christian moral norms, values, commandments and ethical principles will seem like an imposition, and a potentially damaging type of spirituality is the result. On the other hand, when young people develop a sense of their identity as created by God, then the choosing and doing of caring, fair and just behaviours will flow freely from the true self in God. In this context, moral laws, norms and precepts have a crucial place in guiding Christian moral behaviour and attitudes, but only when they are integrated into a healthy Christian spirituality.

The Catholic primary religious education curriculum: some key points of emphasis

In the Catholic school, moral education occurs within the broader context of religious education and the Christian ethos of the school. This is because of the intimate connections between religious convictions, moral reflection and action, and spiritual and liturgical practices. Catholic teachers invite children to reflect on their moral experiences, to make moral judgements and to respond morally *in light of Christian faith.* This is why the formal curriculum for moral education in Catholic primary schools is offered as part of an integrated Religious Education Curriculum. The 'Christian Morality' strand is never taught in isolation from the other strands of the curriculum: Christian faith, the Word of God and Liturgy/Prayer.[12] Keeping this in mind, some of the key points of emphasis in the 'Christian Morality' strand are discussed below.

Love of God as the basis for morality

In the Catholic school morality is understood as a response to God who has taken the initiative in loving us. Therefore, the child's *experience* of the love of God for her is crucial for the development of a healthy Christian morality. As Richard Gula explains:

> For Christians the fact that God loves us is the ultimate truth and the basis on which we live our lives. To know that God loves us and cares for each one in his or her particular life, enables us to reach our fullest potential. The first goal therefore of any Christian moral education is to enable children to experience the love of God for them. We do so by teaching them that all of life is lived in the presence of God, is a response to God, and that everything that they do and say has a meaning and value in relation to God's love.[13]

The world-renowned catechist Sofia Cavalletti is particularly clear on the importance of young children being allowed to enjoy their relationship with God before introducing them to moral principles, norms or rules. She notes:

> Too often we obscure or actually impede this enjoyment
> with preoccupations – especially those that are
> moralistic in character …. If we put too great or too early
> an emphasis on man's (sic) response, our attention will
> be centered on man rather than on God and then strain
> will prevail in our relationship with God.[14]

In a similar vein, the experienced religious educator Francoise Darcy-Berube cautions against the use of God as a 'means' in the moral formation of young children. Instead, the child should be enabled to experience 'the serene enjoyment of God's love':

> Christian morality is about love and the search for
> happiness. – genuine Christian morality is about trusting
> enough in God's love that we accept to search for our
> happiness in responding to God's invitation to love as
> Jesus did. The more the young child will have had the
> time and opportunity to 'fall in love' with God and enjoy
> the relationship with God, the better chance there is that
> the older child's moral response will be 'autonomous
> and genuine'. An autonomous and genuine response
> comes from within the heart where the Spirit of God
> is active. It is opposed to a fearful and guilt-ridden
> obedience to an external law imposed by adults often in
> the name of God.[15]

Human dignity and sacredness

A key task of Catholic moral education at primary level is to introduce children to their identity and dignity as creatures made in the image and likeness of God and of the invitation to respond to the dignity of every other human being created by God. As John Dwyer has explained, the Christian view of the person is distinguished from secular ethical approaches by the fact that Christians see 'human dignity as flowing from the person's relationship with God and not as the result of some quality that human beings possess independently'.[16]

Francoise Darcy-Berube suggests that a holistic early moral education respects the dignity of the child when it encourages children to discover 'different qualities of joy'. Firstly, children should be enabled to experience the joy of discovering their special talents and qualities. Developing a positive self-image, a love and appreciation of oneself, is of foundational importance for children's healthy development. Secondly, children should be helped to 'discover the joy of progressing, of overcoming difficulties or fears, of developing their talents, to reinforce their self-confidence'. In this regard, Darcy-Berube cautions against 'pushing the child to be better than everyone else'.[17] Thirdly, when we sense the child is ready for it, perhaps around age six depending on the child, children should be helped to discover 'the special joy of loving, of giving joy to others even when it requires a special effort, or if it is at the expense of our pleasure .... We will thus have begun to awaken in the child ... [a] ... eucharistic attitude, a willingness to give our life and not only live our life'.[18]

As young children develop a healthy sense of self-identity and of their own sacredness and goodness they are also taught to appreciate the dignity and sacredness of all other persons created by God. We are not self-sufficient individuals; nor are we simply social constructs that have no common human nature or substance. Instead, we are made to be in relationship with one another: self-discovery and true happiness arise when we transcend our own concerns and reach out to each other. In the Catholic school, therefore, service of others and profound respect for the humanity of every person is presented as the ethical ideal.

The Christian tradition of welcoming the stranger and the ethical imperative of surrender to the poor and suffering other in our midst has its roots in Jewish tradition. James C. Conroy offers a helpful description of this Jewish-Christian ethic of hospitality as follows (emphasis mine):

> This particular religious duty ... stands in contrast to the secular conceit of tolerance — that is, tolerance with its roots in John Locke's (1690) desire to have those of contesting attachments live harmoniously together. Locke's and subsequent accounts within the liberal, secular tradition offer an ungenerous and minimalist account dominated by securing peace for oneself, whereas a refurbished account of the historical understanding of *hospitality as a sacred obligation to the other*, irrespective of one's personal dispositions, offers a quite radical alternative. This radical difference lies in the treating of others entirely as ends, ... a view of the other that is committed to maintaining their otherness solely because it is theirs and not because it may lead to some kind of social peace deemed to be in the interests of the majority.[19]

This ethical imperative which requires us to move beyond individualism and egocentricity to treat others as ends and not as means, is one reason why prayer is an essential part of moral living for a Christian. This is because prayer teaches us how to relinquish the ego-centric self and become open to others. Indeed, when we encounter Jesus Christ in prayer we find ourselves increasingly drawn to care for the poor and suffering people in our midst. Children's experience of prayer develops their relationship with Christ from which all moral action flows.

Human freedom and responsibility

Christians believe that every human person is free and that we are responsible for our moral actions and decisions. However the way freedom is understood in Catholic morality differs from the way freedom is understood in secular moralities. Catholics understand that every human being is endowed with a spiritual and immortal soul, with intellect and free will. By virtue of their souls and their powers of reason and free will, they can escape the determination of physics and exercise freedom.[20] This capacity to exercise free will is what distinguishes humanity from the rest of creation. Russell Connors and Patrick McCormick explain that 'we humans have a threefold freedom to make choices about the kinds of persons we will become, the kinds of things we will do, and the kinds of communities we will fashion for ourselves and our children'.[21]

So while Christians value freedom they understand that true freedom is the freedom to be in union with God's actions and purposes in the world. This is a freedom that responds to God's unconditional gift of Godself, God's offer of a covenant relationship with us to which we respond in living ethically. John Sullivan clarifies that freedom is related more to personhood than to individuality by Christians:

Christian freedom should not be confused with the individualism and self-expression that are encouraged in our contemporary culture. In such a context, freedom means removal of constraints and self-sufficiency. ... Christian freedom, in contrast, takes seriously our social nature, our interdependence and our duty to preserve the common good; it expects our decisions to be taken in the light of an informed conscience and guided by a truth which comes from beyond ourselves. A Christian interprets freedom as best developed in a theonomous and Christocentric way. We are oriented to salvation. We do not thrive by emphasising our autonomy. A Christian believes that humans flourish best only by accepting God's authoritative guidance and grace and by following the path of discipleship laid down by Jesus the Christ and witnessed to in the New Testament. This kind of freedom, far from inducing passivity, narrowness or exclusiveness on the part of learners, requires from them an active receptivity, an openness to the unfamiliar, an energetic engagement with the world and an inclusive reaching out to others.[22]

Some important skills of the Catholic moral curriculum which lay the foundations for a mature Christian understanding of freedom include: helping children to understand that they are accountable for their decisions and responsible for their words and actions; enabling children to reflect on their freedom to make choices and the relationship between choice and consequences; teaching children to recognise their conscience and to develop the skill of making moral decisions with a conscience informed in light of the Word of God, the teachings of the Church and the inspiration of the Holy Spirit; and enabling children to learn about the importance of sacraments and prayer as the basis for using their freedom responsibly.

Morality as life in community

In Catholic schools, moral life is presented as life lived in a community of people who are called to live in loving, respectful, relationship with God, other human persons and the whole of creation. Many writers on moral education emphasise the importance of the school 'ethos', 'climate', 'culture', 'atmosphere' or 'characteristic spirit' in enabling children to form healthy human relationships and to develop good character.[23] Josephine Russell points out that there is a greater awareness today of the role of the 'hidden curriculum' on character development, noting that 'some believe that the indirect methods of teaching character are perhaps more beneficial than traditional curricula based approaches.'[24] This recognises that moral or ethical education in all schools is delivered through every aspect of the school day, not just through the formal moral education curriculum.

Research studies abound which highlight the importance of caring school communities, and of secure attachment to teachers who have clear values, as a basis for prosocial and moral development.[25] Darcia Narvaez discusses the pivotal role played by moral communities which strengthen the connections among children's life spaces – home, school, and community – at various levels:

> Children who live with coordinated systems are adaptationally advantaged (Benson, Leffert, Scales, & Blyth, 1998). The type of person a child becomes is determined in large part by the dynamic interaction

among community, family and culture. Caring communities with high expectations and involved adults are more likely to raise morally engaged citizens.[26]

While it is important not to overstate the extent to which Irish Catholic primary schools are simply an extension of a Christian moral orientation of the families where their students come from, there tends to be broad support on the part of Christian parents for a stable and coherent Christian ethical upbringing for their child, as well as a mature recognition that it is not possible to educate their child ethically apart from his or her religion.

Modelling and motivation

Research into the moral development of small children suggests an educational approach that moves from caring relationships in a distinctive and supportive community to gradual development of freedom, autonomy and growing self-identity as the child gets older.[27] So children probably learn best how to be moral in a *Christian* way, by experiencing Christian values, attitudes and behaviours on a day-to-day basis in the school, and by being in relationship with authoritative teachers and others who treat them with respect, compassion, justice and love. This means that modelling of Christian virtues, values and dispositions by adults is probably more important than anything children might learn through the formal moral education curriculum.

Catholic moral education offers children the image of Jesus as *the* greatest model of character, *the* greatest exemplar of how to live a human life. Children are also invited to explore the stories of holy people and saints who lived in the way of Jesus and of contemporary Christians who are inspired by the life of Jesus to work for love and justice all over the world.

It's one thing to know what is right; it's another thing to do it. Moral education is not just about helping children to reason morally and to know right from wrong. Children can have a lot of information and have a lot of cognitive skills and still make the wrong choice. They have to be motivated to do the right thing and have the courage to actually do it. As Roger Straughan notes, 'Teaching children to be moral' is 'a matter of teaching them to *want* to be moral'.[28] The invitation to develop a moral self-identity as a follower or disciple of Jesus provides one important source of moral motivation for children in Catholic schools.

Catholics do good because it is right *and* out of love for Jesus. The ability to feel empathy and compassion for the other person, as Jesus did, is of the utmost importance here. So too is the understanding that all humans are brothers and sisters because we have all been created by God and have a destiny with God in heaven. As Saint Paul says in his Letter to the Romans, 'for the love of Christ urges us on' (2 Cor 5: 14). Since Jesus rose from the dead on Easter Sunday Christians know that their ethical behaviour matters. The success of Jesus' way of compassionate love has been vindicated and will ultimately triumph. The hope offered by the resurrection is that God will ultimately vindicate all those victims of unfair treatment, misfortune, injustice, greed and evil throughout history.

Character formation
Catholic schools encourage a form of moral education in which teachers seek to enable children to develop good

character in the form of specific habitual virtues such as faith, hope, love, compassion, desire for truth, courage, generosity, justice, chastity and forgiveness. Ideally, children are enabled to develop these virtues through habitual practice in a stable environment where home, community and school mirror those virtues and support their practice. As such, moral development in the Catholic school is not understood as a purely natural unfolding or development of children's innate capacities. It is understood rather as a process whereby all the powers of body and soul are disciplined, guided and transformed under a set of Christian moral norms.[29] This has a number of implications for moral education at primary level. Firstly, the development of virtues, habits, emotions, motivation and admirable traits of character is given more emphasis than the development of ethical reasoning and skills of moral debate in Catholic moral education.[30] Secondly, Catholic moral education involves direct teaching of Christian virtues and Christian moral principles (e.g. the love commandments, the ten commandments, the beatitudes), attitudes, dispositions and practices. Children are empowered to understand, evaluate and apply Christian moral precepts, maxims and rules to their own lives.

God's graceful presence and assistance
According to Christian faith, all persons are made in the image and likeness of God but all human persons have been wounded in their nature by original sin, are subject to error and inclined to evil in exercising their freedom.[31] Therefore all persons are in need of salvation by a source beyond themselves. Christ, by his life, death and resurrection, delivered us from sin and enables those who

believe in Him to experience new life in the Holy Spirit. Therefore, for Christians, the call to goodness and to ethical living always demands a response to God's creative and saving actions towards us. In other words, because of our human limitations and fallibility, we need God's grace and forgiveness to enable us to pursue the good and achieve our moral goals. This understanding is very different from those approaches to moral education which convey the idea that a moral utopia can be achieved which ignores human sinfulness, suffering and death.

In the Catholic primary curriculum, children learn that they need God's help to live ethically. The good news is that Jesus gave us his own Spirit who is always with us as we strive to live ethically and authentically. It is in the context of this good news that children are invited to become aware of moral failure and of sin, to accept the need for forgiveness, conversion and faithfulness to the One who has saved us, to appreciate the mercy of God and to understand that learning to live like Jesus did is only possible with the aid of the grace of the Holy Spirit. Furthermore, children learn that the Word of God and the teaching of the Church (and not just their own powers of rational decision making), help them discern right from wrong. Finally, they learn the importance of the Word of God in Sacred Scripture, prayer, asceticism and the sacraments in nurturing their moral lives.

Moral reflection and the development of conscience
The ability to use one's reason to make moral choices is an essential part of moral development. However, approaches to moral education in primary schools differ significantly in the emphasis placed on moral reasoning. The emphasis in Catholic moral education is on teaching children about

the place of the heart (attitudes, emotions and soul), as well as reason, in shaping moral responses. Children are offered opportunities to use their reason in confronting moral problems, to review and evaluate behaviour, to reflect on the reasons for moral precepts, rules and actions, to experience, understand, judge and decide in relation to ethical problems, to apply Christian religious principles, maxims and rules to their own lives and to decide on ethical actions.

The development of ethical reasoning in Catholic moral education coincides with the development of conscience. Children are taught that human persons are obliged to follow the moral law, which urges them to do what is right and avoid what is evil and that this law makes itself heard in their conscience. At the earlier levels of the curriculum conscience is presented as the voice of God which urges us to do what is good and avoid what is evil. At a later stage, children are taught that, in forming their conscience, they are assisted by the Word of God, the gifts of the Holy Spirit, the witness or advice of others and the authoritative teaching of the Church.

Moral reflection and reasoning in Catholic schools takes account of the developmental capacities of the child. As Ian MacMullen explains, young children are not yet developmentally capable of the autonomous reasoning of adults. It is best that they start by learning how to request reasons within the ethical framework provided by the school:

> Initially, ethical reasoning takes the limited form of considering how to apply or interpret fairly concrete principles within a particular ethical system that is transmitted to children but not itself justified to them in rational terms. Only considerably later are children

typically ready for and able to profit from critical reflection on the framework of principles and commitments within which their ethical reasoning capacities were first developed.[32]

This holds true whether the ethical framework is secular (e.g. a human rights framework) or religious (Catholic, Muslim, Jewish, etc.). MacMullen's argument is supported by the findings of cognitive developmental theory: children only gradually develop the kind of logical, abstract and hypothetical thinking necessary for autonomous reasoning.[33] He cites the work of Meira Levinson, who argues that 'very young children ... may well experience confusion and distress if confronted with a plethora of choices too early, or with teachers who tell them that their way of life embodies only one possibility among many'.[34] Thus it is appropriate that the moral education of young children in primary school would be complemented by secondary and university education. At these levels, students can be encouraged to move beyond reasoning within their own religious ethical framework to reflect critically on this framework in relation to other frameworks.

Developing a moral life story in conjunction with the Christian story

Moral behaviour depends on more than moral reasoning, moral judgement and moral beliefs. As Antonio Blasi has pointed out, it depends in part on the importance of moral concerns to our sense of identity and the desire to be faithful to our moral commitments. Blasi has found that we tend to be motivated to act in ways that are consistent with our image of ourselves, our sense of identity.[35] Furthermore, says Blasi, our moral sense and moral motivation is tied up in the *story* or *narrative* we tell about ourselves.[36] In a similar vein, the philosopher Joseph Dunne refers to the 'storied' or 'historical' self, as '...we make sense – or fail to make sense – of our lives by the kind of story we can – or cannot – tell about it'.[37] We human beings cannot help but experience our lives as an ongoing story and part of moral education is discovering the story or stories of which we are a part. As Josephine Russell summarises:

> Moral sense is tied up with my sense of self as a person. If I have established consistency between my judgements and my actions I will see obligations as personally binding and strong affective bonding will strengthen moral motivation. ... Therefore a secure self is a connected self. ... Our concept of selfhood is derived from the unity of a narrative which links us to those around us from birth. In a word, narrative structure is at the core of the formation of the self.[38]

In the Catholic school children are immersed in the narrative of Christian faith as a narrative structure for their self-identity and as an ethical ideal. Scripture stories and other stories of Christian faith which echo the story of salvation become the lens through which children begin to evaluate their moral actions and concerns. John Sullivan explains that, when we adopt a 'story' as a guide for life, it can 'structure our priorities, elicit our energies, sustain our efforts in the face of difficulties and encourage us to co-operate with others who share its vision of embodied ideas'.[39] Connors and McCormick point that stories teach us morality in two ways:

First, by forming and re-forming our personal and communal character, and second by giving concrete directions about how we ought to behave in a particular setting ... on the level of character, stories help to teach us by developing our sympathetic imagination. ... these stories are also, for Christians, the story of who we are, locating us as they do in our most fundamental relationships: with the divine, with our neighbours, and with our own humanity. ... by revealing God and ourselves to us these stories shape our character, making radical demands upon us, not simply by telling us how we should act and what we should do, but by pointing out the sorts of persons and communities we are called to become.[40]

When children engage with the images in Christian story and parable they are invited to open themselves to the possibility of being met by a God who enables them to see the world and order their values in a new way. Christian narratives draw their attention to the holy dimension of all reality, to see the world in its depth as permeated with the presence of God, to see everything and everyone as held in being by love. Religious moral formulations are embedded in a web of character, events, images and symbols.[41] When children listen to a story they enter into the imaginative energy of the story, and so allow the story to organise their experience and their feelings in a new way. They identify with the plot and characters and see how the principles, values and virtues embodied by the characters echo in their own experience. In this way, children are invited to see themselves as participants in an ongoing narrative of both individual and community-based receptivity and responsiveness to God's communication and offer of a covenant relationship.[42]

Social teaching of the Church

Catholic social teaching is a set of principles and guidelines which have emerged over the centuries as Christians have tried to work out in practice how Christian faith affects political, economic and environmental questions. The main areas of Catholic social teaching with which we are concerned in the primary school include development and respect for the environment, the Christian option for the poor, the universal destination of earthly goods, fundamental human rights, peacemaking and reconciliation.[43]

Catholic moral educators aim to help children to have a strong sense of social justice and to contribute to the common good. This means that they are formed in such a way as to respect the identity, culture, history, religion, human rights and especially the suffering and needs of others, conscious that 'we are all really responsible for all'.[44] Catholic schools put a particular emphasis on education for faith that leads to justice, peace and non-violence. Children are invited to study justice issues in the local community such as care of the aged, homelessness, equality issues, poverty, consumerism and the environment. They are also invited to study people and organisations which work for peace and justice in the world (e.g. Trócaire, Red Cross, Catholic Commission for Justice, Peace and Ecology, International Women's Day, Christian non-violence movement, Children Helping Children).

The Catholic curriculum incorporates a development education approach. Through this approach, children are introduced to the concepts of solidarity, the option for the poor, compassion, generosity, inclusion, empathy and responsibility. It is important to note that the vision of justice and social transformation offered by the Catholic school rests on the recognition that we need God's help to bring about this vision.

Human rights
The ethics of Catholic Christianity has a strong tradition of insisting that there are universal and binding moral principles which can be known by human reason, unaided by revelation. Therefore, Catholic educators should be to the forefront in teaching how people of differing religious and non-religious backgrounds can come together in discerning universal ethical principles which can be agreed upon by all.[45]

The discourse of human rights is the dominant moral discourse of our time. It is an important language through which Catholics can converse with others in society about the notion of the human dignity of *every* person, respect for human freedom, the relationship between human freedom and the common good and the need for co-operation between communities in our response to suffering and injustice in the world.[46] The perspective within which human rights discourse is examined in the Catholic school is clarified by the following comment of Ethna Regan:

> Human rights discourse is not simply about what the individual can claim, but about what we have a duty to give to, or protect in, others. Rights thus become an obligation of justice and generosity, a means in pursuit of the common good, a matter not just of strict justice, but also of friendship.[47]

The exercise of rights by individuals is always subject to the limitations of justice and social harmony, and everyone is bound by duties to the communities of which they are a part. Rights are exercised for the sake of the common good rather than as acts of self-expression of radically autonomous individuals who ignore their duties toward others.[48] Furthermore, the language of rights in the Catholic school is always attached to a theological vision whereby Christian children are enabled to recognise that it is in responding to God's love for us that we approach others with compassion and seek their good.

Care for God's creation
In the Catholic school, ecological respect and concern are rooted in a scripturally based theology of creation and related ethical considerations. God creates and gives us the gift of creation to care for and celebrate, and the Christian hope for the final renewal of all creation at the end of time encourages our commitment to cultivate and care for the earth. Children are taught about the unique and special place of human beings in God's creation and that they are invited to become co-creators with God and stewards of God's creation. They are taught about the interconnection of all creation in God and they are encouraged to develop affection, respect and care for all creation as a manifestation of the divine. They are also taught to contemplate creation in all its complexity and beauty and to criticise patterns of consumption that relate to ecological degradation. Children are enabled to understand the concept of eco-sin and to develop an ecological conscience which calls for prophetic challenges to forces destroying the earth. They

will be invited to see that they are called to co-operate with God in counteracting influences that damage or destroy the natural world.

Conclusion

The Christian conception of moral life is always seen in relation to understanding and worship of God.[49] Therefore, Catholic moral education takes account of children's religious identity as created by God and called to be in relationship with God, both here in this world and hereafter for all eternity in heaven. As such, Catholic moral education is always integrated into the overall religious education of the child. Ultimately, Catholic children are invited to develop their moral character by participating in the life and practices, story and vision of the Christian community. The invitation to respond to the love of God for them will ground Catholic children's attitude and approach to issues such as human rights, care for the environment and actions for peace and social justice in the society in which they live.

Questions for reflection

» Examining the moral frameworks in any particular school: what reasons does the framework give for being moral?
» What values or virtues are foregrounded in the moral education in this school?
» What narrative(s) does the school offer for moral self-identity?
» What sources of moral motivation are offered to the child in this school?
» What has the moral framework to say about moral failure, human suffering, human limitations and evil?

Supplementary reading

» Ian MacMullen, 'Education for Autonomy: the Role of Religious Elementary Schools', in *Journal of Philosophy of Education* (2004), 38(4): 601-615.

» Peter Henriot, Edward DeBerri and Michael Schultheis, *Catholic Social Teaching: Our Best Kept Secret* (Maryknoll, NY: Orbis Books, 1989).

» Richard M. Gula, *The Good Life: where morality and spirituality converge* (New York: Paulist Press, 1999).

» Gerald O' Collins, S. J. & Mario Farrugia, S. J., *Catholicism: The Story of Catholic Christianity*. 2nd ed. (Oxford: Oxford University Press, 2015).

Endnotes

1. Donal Murray, *A Special Concern: The Philosophy of Education: a Christian Perspective* (Dublin: Veritas, 1991), 20.
2. Alasdair MacIntyre. *After Virtue: A Study in Moral Theory*, 2nd edn. (Notre Dame/Ind: University of Notre Dame Press, 1984), 216.
3. L. Philip Barnes, *Education, Religion and Diversity: Developing a new model of religious education* (London: Routledge, 2014), 226.
4. Charles Taylor, 'Iris Murdoch and moral philosophy', in Maria Antonaccio and William Schweiker (eds), *Iris Murdoch and the Search for Human Goodness* (Chicago and London: University of Chicago Press, 1996); Charles Taylor, *Sources of the Self: the Making of Modern Identity* (Cambridge, MA: Harvard University Press, 1992).
5. Hanan A. Alexander, 'Autonomy, faith and reason: McLaughlin and Callan on religious initiation', in Graham Haydon (ed.), *Faith in Education: a tribute to Terence McLaughlin* (London: Institute of Education, University of London, 2009), 40–1.
6. Rowan Williams, *Faith in the Public Square* (London: Bloomsbury, 2012), 17.
7. Williams, ibid., 90.
8. Williams, ibid., 90–1.
9. Curtis L. Hancock, *Recovering a Catholic Philosophy of Elementary Education* (Mount Pocono, PA: Newman House Press, 2005), 36–7.
10. Hancock, ibid., 41.
11. Vatican II, *Gaudium et Spes*, (Pastoral Constitution on the Church in the Modern World, 1965), no. 39; Catechism of the Catholic Church, 1042–50.
12. The Christian Morality strand does not purport to contain all of the educational activities and concepts necessary for education in Christian morality at primary level. For example, concepts relating to God's merciful love, the concepts of sin and forgiveness, grace and salvation, the Creed and the Our Father are outlined under the Christian Faith and Liturgy/Prayer strands. Education

in the theological virtues of faith, hope and charity is found throughout the curriculum. Education on the role of the Holy Spirit as a gentle guest and friend who inspires, guides, corrects and strengthens Christian moral life is also found under the Christian Faith strand. The ecclesial dimension of moral life is also emphasised in other areas of the curriculum. The importance of an individual's moral decisions for salvation is also treated under eschatology (Christian Faith strand).

13. Richard M. Gula, *The Good Life: Where Morality and Spirituality Converge* (New York/Mahwah: Paulist Press, 1999), 2.

14. Sofia Cavalletti, *The Religious Potential of the Child: the description of an experience with children from ages three to six* (New York/Ramsey: Paulist Press, 1983).

15. Francoise Darcy-Berube, *Religious Education at a Crossroads* (New York/ Mahwah: Paulist Press, 1995), 126–77.

16. John Dwyer, 'Person, Dignity of', in Judith. A. Dwyer and Elizabeth L. Montgomery (eds), *The New Dictionary of Catholic Social Thought* (Collegeville, Minnesota, Liturgical Press, 1994), 724.

17. Francoise Darcy-Berube, ibid., 127–9.

18. Darcy-Berube, ibid., 131.

19. James C. Conroy, 'Religious Schooling and the Formation of Character', in Hanan A. Alexander and Ayman K. Agbaria (eds), *Commitment, Character, and Citizenship: Religious Education in a Liberal Democracy* (London: Routledge, 2012), 94.

20. Catechism of the Catholic Church, nos 1703, 1705, 1711, 1712.

21. Russell B. Connors, Jr. and Patrick T. McCormick, *Character, Choices & Community* (New York/Mahwah: Paulist Press, 1998), 9.

22. John Sullivan, *Catholic Education: Distinctive and Inclusive* (Dordrecht: Kluwer Academic Publishers, 2001), 119–20.

23. For an overview of some of the research literature here, see Josephine Russell, *How Children Become Moral Selves: building character and promoting citizenship in education* (Brighton/Portland: Sussex Academic Press, 2007), 94.

24. Russell, ibid., 95.

25. See Marvin W. Berkowitz and Melinda Bier, 'The Interpersonal Roots of Character Education', in Daniel K. Lapsley and F. Clark Power (eds), *Character Psychology and Character Education* (Notre Dame: Indiana: University of Notre Dame Press, 2005), 268–85 for a summary of some research studies on this theme.

26. Darcia Narvaez, 'Human Flourishing and Moral Development: Cognitive and Neurobiological Perspectives of Virtue Development', in Larry P. Nucci and Darcia Narvaez (eds), *Handbook of Moral and Character Education* (New York/London: Routledge, 2008), 320.

27. G. Nunner-Winkler, 'Development of Moral Understanding and Moral Motivation' in F. E. Weinert and W. Schneider (eds), *Individual Development from 3 to 12* (Cambridge: Cambridge University Press, 1999), 252–90; Antonio Blasi, 'Moral Understanding and the Moral Personality: The Process of Moral Integration' in W. M. Kurtines and J. L. Gewirtz (eds), *Moral Development: an Introduction* (Boston: Allyn & Bacon, 1995), 229–53; Carolyn Hildebrandt and Betty Zan, 'Constructivist Approaches to Moral Education in Early Childhood'

in Nucci and Narvaez (eds), ibid., 366; Larry P. Nucci, 'Social Cognitive Domain Theory and Moral Education' in Nucci and Narvaez (eds), ibid., 295–96.

28. Roger Straughan, *Can We Teach Children to be Good?* (Bristol: Open University Press, 1988), 111.

29. For a more in-depth reflection on the idea that more than self-realisation is required for healthy growth of character see Sullivan, *Catholic Education*, 112ff.

30. Hancock, Ibid., 129.

31. Catechism of the Catholic Church, no. 1714.

32. Ian MacMullen, 'Education for Autonomy: the Role of Religious Elementary Schools', in *Journal of Philosophy of Education* (2004), 38(4): 605.

33. See a survey of the research which confirms that most children in primary schools are incapable of detachment from their own point of view and adopting a viewpoint contrary to their own in W. K. Kay, 'Phenomenology, religious education, and Piaget', *Religion* (1997), 27(3): 275–83 .

34. Levinson, Meira, *The Demands of Liberal Education* (Oxford :Oxford University press, 1999), 95, cited in MacMullen, 'Education of Autonomy', 602.

35. Antonio Blasi, 'The Development of Identity: Some Implications for Moral Functioning' in Gil G. Noam and Thomas E. Wren (eds), *The Moral Self* (Cambridge, MA: The MIT Press, 1993), 99.

36. Josephine Russell, ibid., 51 Antonio Blasi, 'Neither personality nor cognition: an alternative approach to the nature of the self', in Cynthia Lightfoot, Chris Lalonde, & Michael Chandler (eds), *Changing Conceptions of Psychological Life* (Mahwah, NJ: Erlbaum, 2004), 3–26; Blasi, 'Moral Character: a Psychological Approach' in Lapsley and Clark Power (eds), ibid., 67–100.

37. Joseph Dunne, 'Philosophies of the Self and the Scope of Education', in *Papers of the Philosophy of Education Society of Great Britain Conference* (Oxford, 1995), 174.

38. Russell, ibid., 53.

39. Sullivan, ibid., 33.

40. Connors and McCormick, ibid., 82, 94.

41. Kevin Nichols, 'Imagination and Tradition in Religion and Education' in Jeff Astley and Leslie J. Francis (eds), *Christian Theology and Religious Education: Connections and Contributions* (London: SPCK, 1996), 194.

42. Sullivan, ibid., 115.

43. For a fuller outline of all of the dimensions in Catholic Social teaching, see Donal Dorr, 'An Introduction to Catholic Social Teaching' in Anne Hession and Patricia Kieran (eds), *Exploring Theology: Making Sense of the Catholic Tradition* (Dublin: Veritas, 2007), 192–201.

44. Congregation for Catholic Education, *Education Together in Catholic Schools* (2007), no. 44.

45. This is known as the Natural Law. For an explanation of Natural Law in Roman Catholic moral theology, see Richard M. Gula, *Reason Informed by Faith: Foundations of Catholic Morality* (New York; Mahwah: Paulist Press, 1989), Chapters 15 and 16.

46. Encyclicals and conciliar documents which inform the treatment of human rights in the Catholic Preschool and Primary School Curriculum include *Pacem in Terris* (1963), which marked the first systematic treatment of human rights in Catholic social teaching, *Dignitatis Humanae* (The Declaration on Religious Freedom, 1965), which grounds the right to religious freedom in the dignity of

the person, *Gaudium et Spes* (The Pastoral Constitution on the Church in the Modern World, 1965), *Redemptor Hominis* (1979), *Sollicitudo Rei Socialis* (1987), *Catechism of the Catholic Church* (1994) and *Compendium of the Social Doctrine of the Church* (2004).

47. Ethna Regan, 'Human Rights: an Ethical Position of Protective Marginality' in Eoin G. Cassidy (ed.), *Community — Constitution — Ethos: Democratic Values and Citizenship in the Face of Globalization* (Mater Dei Institute, Dublin: The Otior Press, 2008), 87.

48. John Langan, 'Catholicism and Liberalism' in R. Bruce Douglass, Gerald Mara and Henry Richardson (eds), *Liberalism and the Good* (New York: Routledge, 1990), 110–11. I am indebted to John Sullivan, ibid., 148, for this reference.

49. Harold D. Horell, 'The Moral Demands of Contemporary Life and Christian Moral Education' in M. de Souza et al. (eds), *International Handbook of the Religious, Moral and Spiritual Dimensions in Education* (Dordrecht: Springer, 2006), 90.

GLOSSARY

Biblical literacy This term refers to children's developing capacity to appreciate the uniqueness of the Bible as the divinely inspired Word of God and to develop the basic skills needed to listen to Scripture and to read and respond to the Word of God with understanding. Skills of biblical literacy include: understanding biblical metaphors; finding a Scripture reference; reading passages of Scripture with the correct pronunciation and understanding; outlining the structure of the Bible; exploring interpretations of Scripture in the Church; relating a phrase or passage to one's own life using critical faculties and creative imagination.

Bigotry As it relates to religion, bigotry is a state of mind where a person is strongly intolerant of opinions, lifestyles or identities of other people because of their religion or, in some cases, the particular branch of the religion to which they belong (e.g. Protestant v. Catholics). A bigot will tend to be unfairly prejudiced against the other.

Catechesis This term describes the educational process whereby the Good News of the gospel is announced and the faith of the Church is handed on to believers in the Church community. The word *catechesis* comes from the Greek verb, *katéchein*, which means 'to resound', 'to echo' or 'to hand down'. In the Catholic Church, catechesis is currently understood as a sub-category within evangelisation and functions to 'promote and mature initial conversion, educate the convert in the faith and incorporate him (sic) into the Christian community' (*General Directory for Catechesis* GDC, 1997, no. 61). The heart of catechesis is initiation into the way of Jesus and it 'presupposes that the hearer is receiving the Christian message as a salvific reality' (*Religious Dimension of Education in a Catholic School*, 1988, nos. 68–9). Catechesis therefore presumes an initial conversion to Jesus Christ and openness to on-going conversion. Furthermore, there is a clear linkage in catechesis between instruction and sacramental ritual. Catechesis is grounded in the Bible and takes place in the context of worship. Through the experience of learning about the faith, liturgy, morality and prayer, 'catechesis prepares the Christian to live in community and to participate actively in the life and mission of the Church' (GDC, no. 86).

Character Your character is an expression of a reasonably stable set of good and bad habits, attitudes, virtues, beliefs, dispositions and practices that make you up as a person, developed over time, and out of which you respond to all of the situations you encounter in life. Your character is your own unique moral identity and it reflects your basic stance in the world. Your character grows and changes as you make choices that generate new habits, attitudes, virtues, beliefs or practices, and so it becomes possible to speak of the 'development of character' through moral education.

Christian spirituality Christian spirituality was defined by Pope John Paul II as follows: 'In effect, the term spirituality means a mode or form of life in keeping with Christian demands. Spirituality is "life in Christ" and "in the Spirit", which is accepted in faith, expressed in love and inspired by hope, and so becomes the daily life of the Church community. In this sense, by spirituality, which is the goal of conversion, we mean "not a part of life, but the whole of life guided by the Holy Spirit". Among the many elements of spirituality which all Christians must make their own, prayer holds a pre-eminent place. Prayer leads Christians "little by little to acquire a contemplative view of reality, enabling them to recognise God in every moment and in everything; to contemplate God in every person; to seek his will in all that happens" .... Christian spirituality is nourished above all by a constant sacramental life, since the Sacraments are the root and endless source of God's grace which believers need to sustain them on their earthly pilgrimage .... It should also be noted that this spirituality is not opposed to the social responsibilities of the Christian life. On the contrary, in following the path of prayer, believers become more conscious of the Gospel's demands and of their duties towards others.' (John Paul II, Post-Synodal Apostolic Exhortation, *Ecclesia in America*, January 22, 1999, no. 29).

Confessionalism A term used to refer to forms of religious education which have as their goal the religious formation of persons in one particular religion, with a specific emphasis on seeking assent to its specific doctrines or beliefs. The truth of the religion in question is assumed, though this does not preclude critical thought and questioning in the educational process. In the British literature on religious education, faith-based schools are sometimes referred to as confessional schools and 'faith-based religious education' is sometimes referred to as 'confessional religious education'.

Common good The notion of the 'common good' conveys the idea that society is not just a collection of autonomous individuals; it is rather a community of people where all are called to cooperate together for the good of all. In the same way, individual nations are called to work together for the good of the *whole* human race. This idea of 'the common good' plays a central role in Catholic social teaching. A concern for the 'common good' means respecting the human rights and dignity of each person while creating a society where the welfare of the entire community is the goal.

Common school This is a term used in the British literature for a school which is open to all students regardless of differentiating characteristics such as religious, ethnic, class or cultural background. The founding philosophy of such schools is secular. Common schools seek to uphold religious freedom and have been highly supportive of diversity, especially with regard to minority groups in many contemporary liberal democracies. In the Irish context, Educate Together and Community National Schools might be described as types of common school, in that they aim to give equal recognition to the different religious or other life stances of children in the school.

Contemplative prayer This is a form of prayer where one quietens and stills the mind and body so as to become receptive to the communication of God in the silence and depth of one's own heart. The gift of contemplative prayer enables the person to see and respond to God's purposes in the world.

Conversion In a Catholic context, conversion describes the opening of a human person to God's love. It literally means 'to turn around' or 'to change direction'. It is a turning away from sin and selfishness and a re-orientation of one's desires, thought processes and actions towards God. Conversion is first of all a work of the grace of God.

Cultural relativism This term refers to the view that cultures can be evaluated only by those who share the beliefs and values of the particular culture in question. A cultural relativist will claim that all cultures are to be affirmed and that cultures should not be criticised as there is no objective criterion by which they can be evaluated. The question of the truth or value of any particular culture is avoided.

Curriculum This describes any programme of study or training. A distinction can be made between curriculum as content (what needs to be studied) and curriculum as process (educational activities that have intrinsic value, regardless of any visible outcome or product). In *The Catholic Pre-school and Primary School Curriculum* the content is described as 'knowledge and concepts' and the processes are described as 'skills'. The 'skills' are based on a holistic theory of knowing that assumes that the process of coming to 'know' in Christian faith includes cognitive, affective and behavioural dimensions.

Doctrine This refers to what the Church believes, teaches and confesses. Church doctrines are those aspects of Christian teaching which faithfully interpret the meaning of the words and deeds of Christ (e.g. the doctrines of God the Creator, Trinity, Christ, the Holy Spirit and Salvation).

The Church's doctrine expresses the fullness of divine revelation. The first part of the *Catechism of the Catholic Church* – the Profession of Faith – contains a synthesis of the doctrines of faith professed by the Catholic Church, as expressed in the Apostles' Creed and further elaborated by the Nicene-Constantinopolitan Creed.

Ecumenism This refers to dialogue between Christian denominations separated by doctrines, history and practice, with the aim of restoring unity in Christ, in one visible Church.

Ethos This describes the characteristic beliefs, values, spirit and attitudes of an educational community. This ethos becomes the norm for behaviour, styles of leadership, educational practices and decisions. The way of being and acting inspired by the Catholic religious tradition can be termed a Catholic ethos. The way of being and acting inspired by liberal philosophy can be termed a secular ethos.

Ethnographic approach This is a postmodern secular approach to religious education which draws on the discipline of ethnography (particularly ethnographic anthropology) and which applies ethnographic studies of adherents of different religious communities to the curriculum of religious education. Ethnographic approaches enable students to appreciate religions as actually lived and experienced by individuals in different cultural settings. Ethnographic approaches tend to: focus on the representation and interpretation of religions in religious education; avoid presenting religions as discrete systems of belief or cultures; emphasise the internal diversity and flexibility of religions as complex traditions which are continually under reconstruction; privilege individual and local beliefs and expressions of religions over communal beliefs and expressions; and focus on social, political and moral aims of religious education.

Faith-based school See denominational schools and denominational patronage.

Fundamentalism This is the demand for a strict adherence to orthodox theological doctrines or fixed interpretations of sacred texts, which are usually expressed in one cultural language which is seen as superior to any other. Fundamentalists tend to approach sacred texts, dogmas and beliefs in a literal manner and often share a desire to go back to a more or less ideal time from which they think contemporary members of the religion/belief system in question have strayed. Fundamentalists find it difficult to accept that religions are living traditions which are subject to change as a result of new experiences, new interpretations and new realities. As a result they tend not to be open to dialogue with adherents of their own religious/ secular tradition or those of any other religious or secular conviction, whom they consider to be severely misguided. Forms of fundamentalism found in contemporary globalised societies include Christian fundamentalism, Islamic fundamentalism, Buddhist fundamentalism, Hindu fundamentalism, atheistic fundamentalism.

Globalisation This is a word used to describe the way in which cultures, nations, political systems and economic systems all over the world are becoming increasingly interconnected and interdependent. Advances in communications technologies along with improved transportation technologies have led to new connections between the political, economic and social life of all the peoples on this planet. Local experiences and events are influenced by distant events across the world, which in turn are influenced by local events. This compression of the world has coincided with increased consciousness of and reflection on global interconnections and on different cultures within the global whole. Globalisation has created new opportunities for genuine encounter between peoples, cultures and religions. It has also created new instances of injustice, prejudice, marginalisation and inter-religious strife. In short, globalisation has created a completely new environment for the development of human and religious identity at this time.

Grace The Catechism of the Catholic Church defines grace as follows: 'Grace is *favour*, the *free and undeserved* help that God gives us to respond to his call to become children of God, adoptive sons, partakers of the divine nature and of eternal life. Grace is *participation in the life of God*. The grace of Christ is the gratuitous gift that God makes to us of his own life, infused by the Holy Spirit into our soul to heal it of sin and to sanctify it. It is the *sanctifying or deifying* grace received in Baptism. It is in us the source of the work of sanctification'(CCC 1996, 1997, 1999).

Inter-religious (Interfaith) dialogue refers to dialogue between the various religions of the world. The aim is growth in respect and understanding for the purpose of peace and a genuine search for agreement on ethics and moral action. Pope John Paul II defined such dialogue as a way of living in positive relationship with others. The Pontifical Council for Interreligious Dialogue is the central office of the Catholic Church for promoting inter-religious dialogue in accordance with the Second Vatican Council declaration, *Nostra Aetate* (Declaration on the Relation of the Church to non-Christian religions, 1965).

Inter-religious education This involves learning 'about' and 'from' the religious faiths of others, while growing in understanding of one's own religious faith. The goal of such learning is a greater understanding of self and other which enables the development of a rooted and adaptive religious identity capable of healthy inter-religious living in a multi-religious world. Inter-religious education invites students to deepen their awareness and knowledge of difference, to respect the religious traditions and/or beliefs of others, to develop positive attitudes towards people of other faiths, to enter into respectful dialogue with others, and to grow in appreciation of their own religious experience, commitment and beliefs in light of the experiences, commitments and beliefs of others. Inter-religious education is distinguished in some of the literature from 'multi-faith religious education' (often phenomenological in approach) on the basis that multi-faith religious education doesn't necessarily imply that children are invited into *dialogue* with those of other religions/secular convictions.

Impartial When educators treat all religions and secular convictions equally, presenting an unbiased, fair, just and unprejudiced account of religion which doesn't privilege one religion over another, their approach is described as being impartial.

Kingdom (Reign) of God The coming of the Kingdom (Reign) of God was the main focus of Jesus' mission and preaching. It is the central theological symbol for understanding his ministry. As a symbol, the Kingdom of God suggests God's saving power in history. It means that God is present, acting in our lives to bring about salvation for all. As a metaphor, the Kingdom of God expresses God's promise of peace and justice, love and freedom, and fullness of life for all. Jesus' redemptive life, death and resurrection accomplished the coming of the Kingdom. The Church is the beginning and seed of the Kingdom on earth, and the ultimate fulfilment of the Kingdom will be in Jesus' Second Coming at the end of time.

'Learning into religion' This involves learning a religion as a way of life. It is religious formation or nurture which includes learning the beliefs, practices and ethical framework of the religion in question. 'Learning into religion' involves learning the ways of knowing particular to that religion (e.g. bringing faith and reason into dialogue, imaginative and metaphorical thinking, critical enquiry, etc.) and it normally invites the student to align themselves with a distinctive religious community.

'Learning about religion' This includes 'enquiry into and investigation of the nature of religions, their beliefs, teachings and ways of life, sources, practices and forms of expression. It includes the skills of interpretation, analysis and explanation'. It does not imply religious commitment. (*Toledo Guiding Principles*, 45–6).

'Learning from religion' This type of learning is concerned with 'developing students' reflection on and response to their own and others' experiences in the light of their learning about religion. It develops pupils' skills of application, interpretation and evaluation of what they learn about religion'. (*Toledo Guiding Principles*, pp. 45–6).

Liberalism This is a political philosophy or worldview stemming from the Enlightenment, founded on the ideas of liberty and equality. Liberals believe in the ethical primacy of the individual human being over against the pressures of the community and that current societal arrangements can be improved. They also tend to emphasise the moral unity of the human race over local cultural differences. Liberals will tend to exalt the power of reason over revelation and the autonomy and rights of the person over consideration of obedience to authority and/or responsibility to the other. Typical liberal values include: individual liberty and freedom of conscience; equality of respect for all individuals; consistent rationality; principles of impartiality and tolerance; and personal autonomy.

Liberal religious education This is a secular model of religious education that is underpinned by and promotes Enlightenment (modern/liberal political) values in and through religious education. As such it tends to underscore the unity of religions and has as its goal the reduction of religious intolerance and discrimination and the promotion of harmony among adherents of differing religions and other stances for living in society. Proponents of this approach normally support the privatising of religious beliefs and religious practices, and consider that, when religion enters the educational domain, it must conform to the requirements of public reason, public ethics and liberal political goals. Students are taught variants of the following common ideas: that all religions are equal; that religious experience is central to religion (and hence religious doctrines are of less importance); that all religions mediate salvation; that all religions are different but complementary expressions of the divine; and that the purpose of religion is essentially moral. (For the foregoing, see L. Philip Barnes, *Education, Religion and Diversity: Developing a new model of religious education*. London: Routledge, 2014).

Metaphysics This is a branch of philosophy which describes the study of being and of the world around us. It is a fundamental view of the world and of existence. A metaphysical worldview aims to describe the world around us correctly. Is it real? Is there anything beyond physical objects measured by science? Is there such a thing as a soul?

Neutrality This is an idea from liberal philosophy which is applied to religious education in common schools. In this context, teaching with neutrality means that the teacher does not support or promote any of the religions/stances for living in the religious education curriculum. It means a genuine attempt not to privilege one religion/stance for living over another, through educational approaches that, it is claimed, are not aligned with any particular religion or worldview. This approach stems from the idea that the liberal state should not promote any particular conception of the good life and that therefore each religion/stance for living is given an equal place in the public square. The question is whether it is philosophically possible to be completely neutral in one's approach to religious education, as all educational approaches are underpinned by various philosophical, sociological, historical, anthropological and psychological theories. Some commentators have suggested that 'impartial' names better the type of approach desired in common schools. (See the distinction between 'procedural secularism' and 'programmatic secularism' below.)

Parochialism This is a state of mind whereby one has a narrowly restricted perspective or opinion. It suggests an excessive concern with narrow issues in relation to one's own religious group and/or community and an inability to take a more universal perspective both within one's own religion and in light of the multi-religious and global context within which religious identities are developed and sustained.

Patronage This refers to private organisations, institutions or religious denominations which establish schools. Normally, the patron provides the land on which the school is established, oversees the general ethos of the school and appoints the board of management to run the school on a day-to-day basis. The vast majority (96 per cent) of primary schools in Ireland are owned and under the patronage of religious denominations. Other patronage bodies include An Foras Pátrúnachta, Educate Together and the Education and Training Boards.

The following four suggested definitions are printed with permission of Dr. Andrew McGrady, Mater Dei Institute of Education, Dublin City University. Note that, currently, both the Educate Together and Community National Schools describe their patronage model as 'multi-denominational'.

Non-denominational: a school under the patronage of a secular body or a body in which religious communities have no right of membership of a Board of Management and which has an explicitly secular ethos. Such a school should provide for an appropriate form of religious education (learning about religions and beliefs) and nurture, knowledge, understanding and appreciation of the religious, the ethical and the spiritual as part of human development. However it clearly would not provide religious instruction and thus the issue of 'opting-out' of 'religious instruction' does not arise.

Denominational: a school under the patronage or trusteeship of a single religious faith community (e.g. a Catholic national school, a Muslim national school or a voluntary secondary school under the trusteeship of a religious congregation or one of the new lay educational trusts). Such a school provides religious instruction according to the traditions, practices and beliefs of the specified religious community. It should also provide a wider religious education and work with parents of other faith traditions to enable them to provide for religious instruction.

Multi-denominational: a school under the patronage of a body (such as a VEC) in which members of religious communities have a right to sit on a Board of Management. Such a school should also provide a common religious education and should provide for religious instruction.

Inter-denominational: a school under the patronage or trusteeship of more than one religious faith community. Such a school provides a common religious education and should provide for a variety of religious instruction opportunities.

Phenomenological approach This refers to a multi-faith, non-confessional approach to religious education which adopts the vocabulary, procedures, philosophical perspective and the (liberal Protestant) theological assumptions of the phenomenology of religion. The basic assumption is that religion is a unique realm of the sacred (or the divine, or the holy), which finds expression in diverse ways through religious phenomena such as myths, sacred writings, rituals and religious practices. It is also assumed that different religions are basically complementary, that they all mediate truth and salvation and that they all refer to a similar basic universal human experience of encounter with and response to the divine. The phenomenological approach to the study of religion requires that one brackets out one's own presuppositions and pre-understandings in order to gain an empathic understanding or experience of the religion being studied. The approach emphasises the experiential (and hence feeling) dimension of religion as the essence of religion is seen to reside in experience, rather than in belief. Religious language evokes experience of the sacred rather than describing it, as it is thought that religious experience cannot be entirely captured in religious language or conceptual knowledge. The aim of the phenomenological approach is that students would have an ability to describe the cultural grammar of religions, linked with an affective awareness of the non-verbal religious experiences that form the essence of the religions under study. The political goal is that students would be led to appreciate the unity of religions as a basis from which to develop respect for others and reduce religious intolerance.

Pluralism This is the proposal that there is an irreducible number of reasonable values and conceptions of the true nature of the self and of reality and of what constitutes a 'good life'. A pluralist society is one in which there is a variety of different beliefs and meaning systems (interpretations of reality), ethical perspectives, cultures and religions.

Relativism This is the belief, theory or doctrine that judgements of truth and value are not absolute and vary according to the person making the judgement and according to the circumstances of time and place. A relativist will declare that all paths to truth, goodness, and beauty are equally valuable and that there are no objective or universal standards by which to evaluate and adjudicate between them. For example, a relativist might hold that all religions are the same and that they are merely expressions of the same Sacred/Holy/Divine realm, that no-one can truly know. The difficulty with relativism is that, while it respects difference, it considers dialogue impossible. As the Congregation for Catholic Education notes:

'Relativistic "neutrality" … is founded on the value of tolerance, but limits itself to accepting the other person, excluding the possibility of dialogue and recognition of each other in mutual transformation. Such an idea of tolerance, in fact, leads to a substantially passive meaning of relationship with whoever has a different culture. It does not demand that one take an interest in the needs and sufferings of others, nor that their reasons may be heard; there is no self-comparison with their values, and even less sense of developing love for them'. (*Educating to Intercultural Dialogue in Catholic Schools*, no. 22)

Religious literacy This refers to the ability to understand and use, in the person's day-to-day life, a repertoire of practices and/or 'ways of knowing' related to the Christian religion using reading, writing, listening, speaking, viewing, drawing, music, movement, critical and creative thinking, and multimedia texts of traditional and new information and communications technologies. This definition is distinguished from definitions of religious literacy which focus on the cognitive or rational dimension of religious learning to the exclusion of other dimensions.

Religious education This could be described as any educational process by which people are invited to explore the human religious traditions that protect and illuminate the experience of belief in transcendence/the divine, leading to personal and social transformation. Religious education may contribute to the process by which people are nurtured in a particular religion or it may simply aim for greater understanding and appreciation of religions and other stances for living.

Religious instruction This is a legal term used in Irish legal and constitutional contexts to describe education in a single religious tradition with the objective of socialising pupils into the religion and/or strengthening their commitment to it. The term 'religious education' is now the preferred term for confessional as well as non-confessional approaches to the discipline.

Salvation describes the way in which the life, death and resurrection of Jesus has saved the world. In action terms salvation refers to a healing, a bringing to health or a making whole and well. The salvation brought about through Jesus is healing from everything that oppresses human beings. While the primary salvation needed is from personal sin, Jesus also brings about salvation from the social effects of sin in society.

Secular This refers to that which is not connected with religion. The focus is on things of this world, on what is tangible, and on temporal (as opposed to religious) affairs. A secular worldview has its roots in eighteenth-century Enlightenment thought. This view assumes that there is no metaphysical reality (and hence agencies or presences beyond the tangible) and that therefore, truth, goodness and beauty can be sought without reference to anything that transcends the world. A secular school or state is not necessarily opposed to religion, but tries to be religiously 'neutral'.

Secularism This term has two common meanings. First, it can refer to the principle that governments and public institutions should remain separate from religious groups, their beliefs, laws and practices. In this sense the Irish government is a secular organisation. Second, secularism can refer to an ideological stance which aims to create a purely secular society and so attempts to ban religion from the public square. Religions are thereby pushed into the private realm. For the secularist, the authority that depends on revelation cannot be allowed to influence reasoned public debate in society. This view excludes religions from having any say in public debate, which often reduces public debate to instrumental and managerial considerations.

Rowan Williams makes a helpful distinction between **procedural secularism** and **programmatic secularism**: Procedural secularism is described as 'a public policy which declines to give advantage or preference to any one religious body over others'. Programmatic secularism' is the 'ideology that religious beliefs and life stances should be relegated to the private sphere outside a supposedly neutral public order of rational persons, thus thinning out the fabric of public debate and of moral passion'. Rowan Williams, *Faith in the Public Square* (London: Bloomsbury, 2012), 2–3.

Spiral curriculum A spiral curriculum is a curriculum structured on consecutive levels which assumes that concepts and skills are revisited at each level so that children's learning develops in complexity and richness. This means that only the new concepts and skills are outlined for each level, and each level subsumes the work of previous levels.

Tolerance Tolerance can be interpreted to mean putting up with something or someone we disagree with or dislike. It can also be interpreted more positively to mean our acceptance of someone who holds different beliefs or who lives in a different way to us. Some writers distinguish between 'negative tolerance' (the first explanation above) and 'positive tolerance', which may imply active engagement and dialogue with persons with whom we disagree. It is worth noting that an attitude of intolerance does not logically follow from belief in the uniqueness and superiority of one's own religion. One can be tolerant while holding strong disagreements with other people on religious matters. Nor is one obliged to accept the thesis that all religions are equally true, to be genuinely tolerant of the religions or worldviews of others.

Tradition ('to hand over, to give over') This is the living transmission of the message of the gospel in the Catholic Church as well as the contents of the Good News itself that is handed on from generation to generation. It consists of doctrine, sacramental celebration and community life practices and institutions.

Virtue A virtue is a positive trait, habit, attitude, quality, or belief deemed to be morally good and which, regularly practised, enables you to become a good human being on both personal and social levels. The opposite of virtue is vice. Examples of virtues include: the cardinal virtues (justice, prudence, temperance and fortitude); the theological virtues (faith, hope and charity); gratefulness; diligence; patience; kindness; openness; hospitality; compassion and generosity.

Worldview A worldview outlines a framework of beliefs about the nature, purpose and meaning of human life, through which individuals or groups interpret and interact with the world. Each worldview contains a claim about reality and the place of human beings in it. Your worldview will contain answers to the following questions: Can we know reality? Is there anything beyond the tangible? Is there a God? Do human beings have immortal souls? Why are we here? What happens when we die?